Matt Makes a Run
for the Border

Matt Makes a Run for the Border

Recipes and Tales from a Tex-Mex Chef

MATT MARTINEZ JR.
AND STEVE PATE

LEBHAR-FRIEDMAN BOOKS
NEW YORK · CHICAGO · LOS ANGELES · LONDON · PARIS · TOKYO

LEBHAR-FRIEDMAN BOOKS
A company of Lebhar-Friedman, Inc.
425 Park Avenue
New York, New York 10022

LIBRARY OF CONGRESS CATALOGING-IN-PUBLICATION DATA
Martinez, Matt.
Matt makes a run for the border : recipes and tales from
a Tex-Mex chef / Matt Martinez Jr. and Steve Pate.
    p. cm.
Includes index.
ISBN 0-86730-768-4 (cloth)
1. Cookery, American—Southwestern style. 2. Mexican American cookery. I. Pate, Steve. II. Title.
TX715.2.S69M32 2000
641.5979—dc21   99-29950
                                                 CIP

BOOK DESIGN AND COMPOSITION BY KEVIN HANEK
SET IN ITC MENDOZA AND FF SCALA SANS

Manufactured in the United States of America on acid-free paper
10 9 8 7 6 5 4 3 2 1

Visit our Web site at lfbooks.com

VOLUME DISCOUNTS
This book makes a great gift and incentive. Call (212) 756-5240 for information or volume discounts.

Contents

ACKNOWLEDGMENTS vii

INTRODUCTION ix

CHAPTER ONE
Appetizers 1

CHAPTER TWO
Soups, Chilis, Stews, Gumbos, and Stocks 17

CHAPTER THREE
Side Dishes 47

CHAPTER FOUR
Main Courses 71

CHAPTER FIVE
Toppings and Sauces 121

CHAPTER SIX
Breads 147

CHAPTER SEVEN
Drinks and Desserts 161

INDEX 183

Acknowledgments

Muchas gracias to this book's many contributors, particularly photographers Tara McLeish, Polly Mullen, and Pat Stowers; Kate McCoy, for taking down a large majority of the recipes and supplying a recipe of charm along the way; Lizzie Ashworth, for taking down recipes while managing Matt's restaurants; Linda Bebee and the Texas Beef Council, for kind help and wonderful recipes; New Mexico ranchers Larry and Virginia Wright, for regaling Matt as they cooked in the woods; Kirk Rogers, bartender at Matt's No Place, for substantial assistance on the coffee drinks and his late-night influence on this entire process; Bill Morgan and Louie Canelakes, our noble spell-checkers; Matt's children (good recipes, Marco) and Matt's mother, Janie Martinez, whose fingerprints were all over the manuscript; Dallas artist Rick Timmons, for his loyal support and artistic input; and, quite naturally, Matt's wife Estella, for putting up with Matt's culinary mistakes (which are very few, by the way). Many thanks as well to our agent, Janet Manus, and the fine folks at Lebhar-Friedman Books, most notably Paul Frumkin, Joseph Mills, and Frank Scatoni.

The Art of the Meal, According to Matt

I'VE NEVER BEEN ALL THAT WILD ABOUT BUZZARDS, and this cookbook is far too user-friendly to include a buzzard recipe—even a stew. But I do know folks who believe I can cook durn near anything and make it come out tasty—which is what caused the buzzard incident in the first place.

Our cast of characters in this story includes six of my favorite hunting buddies—and me, of course. I'd tell you their names but they might get mad. We all have a hard time remembering names anyway.

Over the past 20 years, I've sat around a few campfires and heard my fellow hunters describe in detail one particular trip. It's all I can do to hold in my ol' belly enough to prevent the laughter from bouncing up and down off my belt buckle and knocking me out.

Let's just say I feel a moral obligation to set the record straight, so here it is . . .

THE REAL BUZZARD-STEW HUNTING TRIP

The weather that early December day was Rod Serling *Twilight Zone* gloomy, featuring a heavy fog that hung over the Texas Hill Country like a nosy neighbor.

I was in my prime—my early 30s—but the cedar in the air had caused my sinuses to kick up. My nose was so clogged, my buddies beat me out of Austin by an hour or three. At dusk, I was just closing the gate to the deer lease when a flock of big ol' turkeys came waddling up.

I went ahead and harvested the chubby one in the rear of the pack with my .38, took him to camp, showed him off while saying my howdies to everyone, then plucked him and cleaned him good.

That night, I told the guys, "The way my eyes are running, I think I'll hold off hunting for a day. Ya'll go ahead in the morning. I'll stay behind and cook some turkey *mole* and a big ol' pot of beans. Everything oughta be ready by the time you return."

Nobody put up much of an argument, and sure enough I had everything cooked up by ten the next morning. But the miserable weather was so deer-hunting good, the gang stayed out longer than expected.

So I sat on the back porch of our cabin and poured myself a few doses of my personal sinus medicine from a bottle of Jack Daniel's whiskey.

I was beginning to feel fairly medicated when I spotted a buzzard resting on the limb of a dead oak tree maybe fifty yards into the mist.

The buzzard seemed to have taken a few nips from his own bottle the way he kept wobbling from side to side, trying to maintain his balance on the limb. One wing would fly up, then a few seconds later the other wing would flutter, and the buzzard seemed to cling to the limb by one leg, like a drunken sailor on a weekend pass.

About the time I was beginning to lose interest, the buzzard flopped to the ground with a thud and lay there deader than Waco on a Monday night.

I'd never seen a drunken buzzard before, but I'd also never seen one simply fall over and die.

Everything having a purpose, I grabbed the camp axe and removed the buzzard's ugly head and feet, then plucked the feathers. I tossed the head and wings and claws into a paper sack, buried the rest of the buzzard in a small hole, then dampened the bottom of the sack with some water and placed it in a corner of the cabin.

The guys returned from hunting about an hour later, and they were so hungry they wolfed down everything I put on their tin plates.

Ol' Dave finally took enough breaths to look up and ask, "Why ain't you eating, Matt?"

"Aw, I ain't hungry," I said. "Looks like I'm the only one who's not."

Crazy Gus wiped his mouth with his shirtsleeve, rubbed his belly and said, "Matt, you been awfully nice to us fellers. Anything we can do for you in return?"

"Aw, I've already got the turkey in the freezer," I replied. "Can't think of anything."

Gus eyed me suspiciously and said, "I thought *this* was turkey."

"Oh, well, yes, of course," I said, turning my attention back to my medication. After a pause that included some more tortilla sopping on their part, I said, "You know what you could do, since you volunteered . . ."

"You just name it, Matt," said Ol' Dave between smacks.

"There's some trash in that sack over there that needs to be thrown out."

Gus jumped up and bunched the top of the sack together so he could grip it in one hand, but before he reached the door the bottom gave way and out dropped the buzzard head and claws. A few feathers lightly settled nearby.

"Gawd dang!" Ol' Dave bellowed. "Matt just fed us a buzzard!"

All six took to screaming, *"AAAAAGHHHH!!!!"*

Every one of them turned egg-shell white, then several shades of yellow before they all hit the door, still screaming, dancing around the front yard like each had been given a hot foot.

I strolled out on the porch and calmly intoned, "Well, you fellas say I can cook anything. I was just trying to substantiate your theory."

Three of the bunch have hated Thanksgiving ever since.

THE BORDER: WHERE FOOD TRANSCENDS BOUNDARIES

I offer the buzzard story as an introduction to this cookbook for one reason: If you want to make sure you know what you're eating, perhaps it's best you cook it yourself.

This cookbook comes on the boot heels of my first one, *Matt Martinez's Culinary Frontier: A Real Texas Cookbook*, which Doubleday was nice enough to publish in 1997. That one might have been printed sooner, but I kept telling my secretary I didn't know anyone named Doubleday so I didn't bother returning the calls.

Like the first one, this cookbook is aimed right at your belly. The recipes are easy to follow and again support my theory that it's tough to beat the old way.

The first cookbook highlighted many of my favorite traditional Tex-Mex dishes and also paid homage to the cowboy style of cooking "reinvented" by one of my Dallas restaurants, Matt's No Place, and also offered at the Y.O. Ranch restaurant in the West End Historic District of downtown Dallas.

This time, I've decided to pay my respects to our dear neighbors outside the borders of Texas.

Over the past three decades and counting, I've worn out the speedometer in several vans and pickups heading south for Mexico, where I love digging even deeper into my roots. I've also gone west to New Mexico, where the stars shine bright and the fires always glow pretty; north to Oklahoma, where the inner-child of the citizens there has a natural appreciation for my prairie-style cooking; northeast to the hills of Arkansas, where the catfish are running and the bacon is frying; and east to Louisiana, just because I like hanging out with all those crazy Cajuns.

I'm a Tex-Mex freak and not prone to change, but these adjoining "countries" do have their own distinct methods of preparing dishes. I've also borrowed from my family's rich cooking heritage in Austin, San Antonio, and Corpus Christi. Texas is a mighty big state, and a man gets hungry when he's making a run for any border. Among others, you have my mother, Janie Martinez, and the folks at the Texas Beef Council to thank for broadening my horizons.

All I'm doing, as you will see in these pages, is adding my own little touches to the dishes that make my little ol' heart go pitter patter.

MATT: LAST OF THE COOKING BUCKAROOS

It would be an understatement to say I've got cooking in my veins. My paternal grandfather and grandmother, Delfino and Maria Martinez, moved from northern Mexico to Austin, Texas, many years ago and in 1925 opened the city's first Tex-Mex restaurant, El Original (*El O-ree-hee-nal*).

Three decades later, their son (and my father) Matt and his wife Janie opened Matt's El Rancho, one of the greatest institutions of any kind in Texas history. That's where my love for cooking began—at El Rancho, and in the kitchen of Janie's mother, Marie Gaytan.

Throughout my childhood, my daddy was busy overseeing El Rancho, and my mother was always running the kitchen, which left my sisters and me in the care of Granny Gaytan. If there was ever anybody who could make a buzzard taste good, it was Granny Gaytan.

I put in my share of hours at El Rancho, got into my share of mischief along the way, and eventually married the love of my life, a little ol' Corpus Christi girl named Estella. By 1985, our family lit out for Vail, Colorado, where I built the world's largest enchilada while running a restaurant, Matt's Café and Cantina, out of a hotel. (Stay tuned, the tale of the enchilada episode is yet to come . . .)

After about a year in exile, I had a major hankering for Texas, so Estella and I moved our family to Dallas, where I ran the restaurant at Catillion Towers off Preston Road. We were dead broke.

One afternoon I was delivering an order of appetizers to the bar when a banker from Austin spotted me. He said he was having a problem with the tenant of a space he owned in the fancy Plaza of the Americas building in downtown Dallas, and he wondered what I might give for it.

"I got nothing to give," I said.

"Come on by my Dallas office anyway tomorrow morning," he said.

So Estella and I went. Estella was so nervous she stayed in the car and prayed. I took a deep breath, walked into the office and told the guy I needed $5,000 to start my own place. He gave me a form to fill out, and I wrote down that I was bankrupt with no assets. I'd even lost my house in Austin before we headed for Vail.

He never blinked. He gave me $20,000 and the keys to what became Matt's Café and Cantina, right by the ice skating rink in the Plaza of the Americas.

About a year later, I opened the first Matt's Rancho Martinez in East Dallas off Ferguson Road. It was way off the beaten path. Nobody in Dallas knew me, so one day I grabbed the phone with one hand and the Yellow Pages with the other, and called every media outlet listed.

"Pardon me," I said again and again, "but I just ate at this little ol' hideaway on Ferguson Road, and it's the best Mexican food I've ever had. I hear it's being run by some big-time restaurateur out of Austin who's trying to hide out in Dallas. Got any idea who he is?"

Here came the media. I could hear rubber burning two blocks away, as reporters hustled to have the first story.

In no time, we were doing so much volume I needed a bigger place. I landed in the Lakewood Shopping Center, where Matt's Rancho Martinez has remained for 13 years. I added No Place next door in 1993 and have opened six other restaurants since then.

Three had to be sold when they began rudely cutting into my hunting and fishing time and severely curtailing my whiskey drinking. But my family and I still operate Rancho Martinez and No Place.

The Y.O. Ranch restaurant in the Historic West End is still dear to me, and I've also got two more places inside Macy's at Dallas' Galleria Mall—Matt's at Macy's and Matt's Texas Coffee & Mexican Bakery.

Despite all these restaurants, I've done my share of wandering over the years. And my wanderings always take me back to my roots.

Even in my travels to Mexico and the neighboring states of Texas, I've found ways to sprinkle in a little bit of Lone Star soul without corrupting the traditional recipes of each region. That's all I'm introducing to you here—a little bit of Texas and a whole lot of heart.

I'm not here to wean city slickers off their five-course meals with fancy tablecloths. I'm simply asking you to take a little trip with me, through this cookbook, en route to a simpler, happier belly.

The old recipes used by cowboys on the open range—back when people ate what they hunted on the prairie and what they caught in streams and the great Gulf of Mexico—remain the most magical.

So pull up a skillet, your favorite knife, and a fire, and let's have some fun cooking. I promise you won't stumble over a single buzzard along the way.

Matt Makes a Run
for the Border

CHAPTER ONE
Appetizers

WHEN I'M PERFORMING FOR OTHERS in the kitchen, I always like to have appetizers around. That's because I get grumpy when I get hungry. (Everyone enjoys life more with a happy belly.)

There's nothing like a good appetizer and a good cocktail to take the devil right out of me. All of a sudden, I'm wearing an angelic smile. My eyes are twinkling. Sometimes, I can dance around a kitchen like Fred Astaire.

I seem to reach for my gun and my knife a whole lot less when there's a good appetizer around.

Beefy Portabellos

My childhood buddies and I were sitting around one day trying to imagine the absolute worst possible thing a boy could put in his mouth, other than his own foot.

We named raw squash and broccoli and mushrooms and a few other things, and then I told them in all sincerity, "I saw this movie once, and this guy was stuck on a small boat in the middle of the ocean, and he got so hungry he ran his hand into the water and pulled out a fish and ate it right down."

It didn't hurt my story when a couple of my buddies started looking a little pink around the gills. So I swore, "Last thing I'm ever gonna eat in this whole world is a raw fish."

You're probably wondering what raw fish has to do with a Beefy Portabellos recipe. Here it is: If it hadn't been for raw fish, mushrooms would not have finished second.

And something as big as a portabello mushroom was a little more than my digestive tract cared to tackle. Somehow, somewhere along the way, my appetite must have got turned upside down and shaken around, cause I've come out a different thinker.

I've eaten enough raw fish to be accused of being Mr. Sushi on more than one occasion, and my boys break me every time we go to a sushi place.

I never thought there'd come a day when I'd find myself recommending raw fish or mushrooms of any variety. So I'm apologizing up front to all my childhood buddies and hoping this Beefy Portabellos recipe will help them understand.

MAKES 8 SERVINGS

2 tablespoons butter

8 small portabello mushrooms

¹/₄ cup red or yellow bell peppers, finely diced

¹/₂ cup green onions, chopped with tops

2 cups cooked shredded beef (see pp. 74-75)

1 cup shredded Monterey Jack cheese

1 recipe of Stand-By Queso (see p. 56)

¹/₂ cup cilantro (optional)

Melt the butter in a frying pan on low heat. Rinse the portabellos and remove the stems, then chop them finely. Remove the gills from the mushroom caps by scraping with a spoon. Brush the caps with some butter.

Sauté the stems, the bell peppers, and the onions in the remaining butter. Add the shredded beef, and heat thoroughly in the skillet. Remove from the heat and add the shredded cheese onto the mushroom caps. Stuff the shredded beef mixture equally onto the cheesy mushroom caps.

Grill over medium coals for 10 minutes, or heat at 350° for 10 minutes, or until the mushrooms are soft. Serve immediately, smothered with Stand-By Queso and garnished with cilantro leaves.

SERVING SUGGESTION

To make these portabellos a main course, serve two mushroom caps over buttered pasta.

Chipotle Chicken Wings

You can fry these wings or bake them. Or, try them both ways and see which strikes your fancy.

1 cup flour

3 pounds chicken wings, tips removed

salt and pepper to taste

1/2 cup melted butter

3 tablespoons Chipotle Paste (see p. 124)

2 cloves garlic, thinly sliced (optional)

Place the flour in a paper sack. Lightly season the chicken with salt and pepper, then lightly coat with flour by shaking the chicken in the sack.

FRYING

Fry in a skillet at 375° for 5 to 8 minutes, until the wings float and get golden brown. Drain the wings on paper towels. Blend together the melted butter, Chipotle Paste, and garlic. Toss the wings into the mixture, coating the wings on all sides. Serve immediately.

BAKING

Bake the wings at 400° for 20 to 25 minutes, or until the wings are golden brown. Blend together the melted butter, Chipotle Paste, and garlic. Toss the wings into the mixture and serve immediately.

South Austin Po' Boy Crab Cakes

If you're wondering why these are called po' boy crab cakes, the answer's pretty simple: There aren't any crabs in the thing.

MAKES 4 SERVINGS AS AN APPETIZER (2 AS A MAIN DISH)

2 eggs

1 can salmon

1 cup cracker crumbs or bread crumbs

$1/4$ cup white onions, finely chopped

$1/4$ cup celery, finely chopped

1 teaspoon salt

pinch of pepper

$1/4$ cup milk

oil for frying

Beat the eggs in a big bowl, then add all the ingredients except the milk. Add just enough milk to spoon it out so that it easily slides off the spoon.

Place enough oil (of your choice) to cover a quarter-inch or less of a skillet, and get it hot. Spoon the mixture into the hot oil. Brown on both sides and serve immediately.

SERVING SUGGESTION
Serve with ketchup or tartar sauce.

Avocado and Shrimp Pico

This dish is nothing but trouble. It goes down so fast that everybody starts clamoring for more. All of a sudden, your guests are saying to heck with what's to come, and I just hate it when my friends get full too soon.

If you ever have the opportunity to use this pico as a side dish, try it with grilled fish, shrimp, chicken, or anything summery.

But remember: It doesn't keep well. Prepare it within two hours of serving time, and keep it wrapped and fresh.

MAKES 4 TO 6 SERVINGS AS AN APPETIZER (4 AS A SIDE DISH)

2 teaspoons lime juice

3 teaspoons olive oil

2 tablespoons (or to taste) finely chopped jalapeño or serrano chile peppers

salt and pepper to taste

2 cups fresh tomatoes, chopped ¼-inch thick

3 teaspoons finely chopped fresh cilantro

1 teaspoon minced garlic (optional)

1 pound cooked shrimp, any size, chopped ¼-inch thick

1 avocado, peeled and pit removed, chopped ¼-inch thick

In a bowl, combine the lime juice, olive oil, peppers, salt, pepper, tomatoes, cilantro, and garlic (optional). Mix them well and allow to sit for 5 minutes to let the flavors blend.

Mix in the shrimp and avocado.

SERVING SUGGESTION
Serve with chips or crackers. For wraps, serve with lettuce leaves. Whatever you do, dig in!

Avocado Caesar's Salad

I must be feeling guilty again because I'm apprehensive about this recipe.

One night in San Antonio, I was lucky enough to be hanging around Julia Child at a Southwestern cooking demonstration. She hated the fact that certain chefs were bastardizing a dish so classic as the noble Caesar's Salad.

"If you're going to make it different," Julia said, quite emphatically, "call it something else."

Oh, Julia, forgive me. It'll never happen again.

MAKES 4 TO 6 SERVINGS

1 clove garlic, finely chopped

1 small, hot, serrano chile pepper, very finely chopped

1 tablespoon olive oil

1 tablespoon anchovy oil from can

3 tablespoons lemon or lime juice

$1/4$ teaspoon Worcestershire sauce

1 ripe avocado, peeled and pit removed

6-7 cups of hand-torn Romaine lettuce

1 cup croutons

$1/4$ cup grated Parmesan cheese

$1/2$ teaspoon salt

$1/2$ teaspoon white pepper

1 2-ounce can of anchovies

In a mixing bowl, combine the garlic, serrano pepper, olive and anchovy oils, lemon or lime juice, and Worcestershire sauce. Let the mixture sit for 5 to 10 minutes, allowing the flavors to blend.

Add the avocado to the mixture, and fork or whisk until smooth. Add the lettuce and toss until the leaves are thoroughly coated.

Add the croutons, Parmesan cheese, salt, and pepper, and toss again. Serve with anchovies on the side.

Cactus Pod Salad

I've always suspected my mother was smarter than nine out of ten doctors. Long before all these studies proved her correct, Mom knew cactus (nopalitos) had a healing heart.

She was making this Cactus Pod Salad before I got knee-high to her or the cactus.

I strongly recommend it with grilled and barbecued meats. But don't ever use canned nopaolitos; the can adversely affects their taste. Only buy nopalitos in a glass jar. Donia Maris is a good brand, if it's in your neighborhood grocery.

MAKES 4 TO 6 SERVINGS

1 15-ounce jar nopalitos

1/4 cup coarsely chopped fresh tomatoes

2 tablespoons diced pimento

1/2 cup finely chopped green onions (red, yellow, or white is also fine)

1 very finely chopped, fresh anaheim pepper

3 tablespoons finely chopped cilantro

2 tablespoons olive oil

1 tablespoon fresh lemon juice or lime juice

Rinse and thoroughly drain the nopalitos. Toss ingredients together and let them rest at least 1 hour covered and chilled, before serving.

Liver Starters

If you're embarrassed about eating liver in front of others, just spear these Liver Starters with a toothpick and hide them under your coat while munching. Or, wrap 'em in a flour tortilla.

If you're not embarrassed, try them with white bread, lettuce, tomato, onion, and mayonnaise. Or, ladled over a plate of steaming white rice.

MAKES 4 SERVINGS

1 pound chicken livers

$\frac{1}{2}$ teaspoon salt

$\frac{1}{2}$ teaspoon black pepper

2 tablespoons flour

4 strips bacon, in 1-inch squares

2 sliced pickled jalapeños

1 cup coarsely chopped white onions

2 cloves garlic, thinly sliced

1 tablespoon sherry or brandy

1$\frac{1}{2}$ tablespoons light soy sauce (Kikkoman works best)

1 tablespoon vinegar

Thoroughly wash the liver in cold water and drain.

Mix the salt, pepper, and flour. Sprinkle the mix over the liver until the liver is thoroughly covered.

In a large skillet, fry the bacon on moderate heat until it starts to change color. Add the liver and cook for 3 to 4 minutes.

Add the jalapeños, onions, and garlic, and continue to cook for 3 to 4 minutes, scraping and loosening all the goodness as you go until the liver is done.

You can check the liver by cutting into a plump piece. If the inside is not red, the meat is ready.

Add the sherry or brandy, soy sauce, and vinegar.

Toss for a minute or two.

SERVING SUGGESTION

Don't forget about the toothpick, tortilla, lettuce leaves, or steamed rice.

Stuffed Avocado with Shrimp

My mom and I don't have to see eye-to-eye on everything. She likes to drizzle French dressing over the top of this appetizer and garnish with a green olive and onion rings. I like mine with chips or crackers, with a salt shaker close by, in case I want to further enhance the avocado.

MAKES 2 SERVINGS

1 cup cooked shelled shrimp, any size

2 tablespoons mayonnaise

1 tablespoon sour cream

¼ cup celery

1 tablespoon lemon juice

salt and pepper to taste

1 avocado, peeled and pit removed, sliced in half

2 cups chopped fresh lettuce

In a large bowl, thoroughly mix all the ingredients except the avocado and lettuce. Salt and pepper to taste.

Place the avocado halves "pit" side up on the lettuce, and heap the mixture on top of the avocado.

Marinated Shrimp

Marinated Shrimp is a wonderful appetizer or side dish for any seafood entree. It goes well with cocktails, too.

1 pound cleaned, cooked shrimp (approximately 20–30 small to medium shrimp)

$^1\!/_2$ cup lime juice

$^1\!/_4$ cup olive oil

2 cloves garlic, thinly sliced

$^1\!/_4$ teaspoon black pepper

$^1\!/_4$ teaspoon crushed leafy oregano (Mexican oregano works best)

1 cup coarsely chopped white onions

1 thinly sliced jalapeño pepper

1 $^1\!/_2$ teaspoons salt

1 teaspoon sugar

$^1\!/_4$ cup chopped cilantro

black pepper to taste

Combine all the ingredients. Refrigerate for 2 to 3 hours.

Serve fresh and cold.

Skillet Scampi Texas Style

A good cast-iron skillet really makes this recipe happen. You're missing out on some great cooking if you don't have a cast-iron skillet.

I could cook exclusively with a cast-iron skillet. The more you cook in one, the better it gets. You take care of your skillet; it'll take care of you. I've never had one flake off. It's the most consistent cooking surface I've ever found. A dog might be hard to top for a best friend, but a good skillet runs a close second.

MAKES 6 TO 8 SERVINGS

2 pounds headless shrimp with shells (about 40 medium shrimp)

$1/4$ cup finely chopped parsley

1 cup melted butter

4 cloves garlic, chopped

1 cup extra virgin olive oil

8 peppercorns

1 teaspoon salt

6 dried chile japones (Japanese peppers)

Rinse the shrimp in cold water and pat them dry with a towel.

Combine the parsley, melted butter, and garlic. Set aside.

Heat the olive oil in a skillet on high. When the oil spits back with water drops (in other words, when it pops), it's ready.

Sauté the peppercorns, salt, and japones in the skillet for 1 minute.

Add the shrimp, and sauté for $2^{1}/_{2}$ to 3 minutes. Add the buttery mixture, and continue to cook for 1 more minute.

SERVING SUGGESTION

Place the scampi on a warm serving platter, and attack with good, crusty bread. Have a stack of napkins nearby, and start shelling and dipping in the butter sauce.

Green Tomatillo Gorditas

You'll notice a couple of Gorditas recipes in the bread section. They're a combo bread/appetizer. These take on a tamale flavor. I usually end up making more than one batch.

MAKES 4 TO 6 SERVINGS

oil for frying

1/4 cup shortening

2 cups dry masa for making tortillas

1/2 teaspoon salt

1 cup shredded meat (beef, pork, or chicken)

1 8-ounce can green tomatillo sauce

1/2 cup water

Add enough grease or oil to fill your favorite skillet 1/4-inch deep.

Combine the shortening, dry masa, and the salt, and blend thoroughly. Add the shredded meat. Toss and blend.

Add the tomatillo sauce and the water.

Form 16 little balls. Flatten the balls in the palms of your hands to approximately 1/4-inch thick. Drop into the hot grease or lard, and brown on both sides.

Drain on paper towels.

Keep them warm by wrapping them in a cloth.

These taste like miniature fried tamales. They are good with queso.

Chicken Gizzards

I like cooking Chicken Gizzards outdoors as a prelude to a good fish fry. It's a nice way to reward the cooking crew. A little Tabasco sauce or your favorite Cajun hot sauce on top is tasty.

MAKES 4 TO 6 SERVINGS

2 pounds chicken gizzards

1½ teaspoons salt

¾ teaspoon black pepper

½ teaspoon granulated garlic

2 cups flour

1 tablespoon cornstarch

2 eggs

½ cup milk

hot sauce (optional)

Pour 2 quarts of water into a large stockpot. Thoroughly rinse the gizzards, and add them to the pot. Bring the water to a boil, and cook the gizzards until they are tender. Remove the gizzards from the stockpot, and let them cool.

Combine all the dry ingredients except the cornstarch and set this mixture aside.

Combine the cornstarch, eggs, and the milk. Whisk thoroughly. Add the tender, cooked gizzards to the egg mixture, and toss them until they are thoroughly coated.

Place the dry mixture inside a large Ziploc or a medium paper bag. Place 6 to 8 gizzards at a time inside the bag. Shake the bag to thoroughly coat the gizzards in the dry mixture.

Drop the gizzards in a deep fat fryer, being careful not to overcrowd, so the temperature in the fryer will remain consistent and not drop. Fry the gizzards to a golden brown. You will know they are ready to remove from the fryer when the gizzards float to the top.

Lay the gizzards on an absorbent paper towel to drain.

These will be the most tender, juiciest gizzards you have ever tasted. They are excellent when enhanced with hot sauce.

Chicken Livers

I love it when people don't like Chicken Livers because that means there's more for me.

2 pounds chicken livers

1½ teaspoons salt

¾ teaspoon black pepper

½ teaspoon granulated garlic

2 cups flour

1 tablespoon cornstarch

2 eggs

½ cup milk

hot sauce (optional)

Pour 2 quarts of water into a large stockpot. Rinse the livers and add them to the pot. Bring the water to a boil and rapidly boil the livers for 2 minutes. Remove the livers from the stockpot, and let them cool.

Combine all the dry ingredients except the cornstarch, and set this mixture aside.

Combine the cornstarch, eggs, and the milk. Whisk thoroughly. Add the cooked livers to the egg mixture, and toss or stir them until they are thoroughly coated.

Place the dry mixture inside a large Ziploc or a medium paper bag. Place 6 to 8 livers at a time inside the bag. Shake the bag to thoroughly coat the livers in the dry mixture.

Drop the livers in a deep fat fryer, being careful not to overcrowd, so the temperature in the fryer will remain consistent and not drop. Fry the livers to a golden brown. You will know they are ready to remove from the fryer when the livers float to the top.

Lay the livers on an absorbent paper towel to drain.

These will be the juiciest livers you have ever tasted. They are excellent when you douse them with hot sauce.

CHAPTER TWO

Soups, Chilis, Stews, Gumbos, and Stocks

GRANTED, THERE IS AN OBVIOUS ART to preparing soups, chilis, stews, gumbos, and stocks. But it's not an exact one.

Therefore, you do not have to stick to rigid guidelines. Think of these recipes as road maps taking you from start to finish, but know that you can take a longer or shorter route and still reach your destination.

Although no gumbos or chilis are ever the same, I've found it's incredibly helpful to take notes as I concoct my brews. Then, after we've eaten up everything, I take more notes about what I should and should not have done.

Maybe I need to remind myself to increase or decrease a particular spice. Maybe I should have used a larger pot. Or gone with a different stock.

These simple notes—write them in the margins of the book, if you please—will allow you to get so much better so much quicker. That way, you don't have to feel like you're inventing the wheel each time.

Sopa de Fideo (Vermicelli)

My granny Gaytan made fideo three or four times a week when I was a boy. Sometimes she added a little chicken, sometimes beef, sometimes just a bowl of beans on the side. It kept me full of energy and prevented me from burning out while in full pursuit of mischief.

Fideo is very easy to make. My children like to mix in a few pintos. But beware: Vermicelli is so fine it burns easily. You must keep an eye on it while cooking.

MAKES 3 TO 4 SERVINGS

1 tablespoon vegetable oil

1 5-ounce box vermicelli (Use finest possible)

½ teaspoon cumin

½ teaspoon salt

½ teaspoon pepper

2 cups chicken stock (see p. 44)

1 clove garlic, mashed

1 cup finely chopped medium tomatoes

½ cup grated cheese of your choice

Heat the oil in a large skillet over low heat.

Brown the vermicelli for 2 to 3 minutes. Be careful not to burn the vermicelli; cook until it is wheat-brown, then add the cumin, salt, and pepper.

In another saucepan, bring the chicken stock, garlic, and tomatoes to a boil. Cover and simmer for 10 minutes.

Add the vermicelli to the broth, breaking up the twists with a spoon in the process. Cover the pan and cook over low heat for 10 more minutes.

Add salt and pepper as needed. Serve immediately with your favorite grated cheese sprinkled over the top.

Trail Blazin' Beef Soup

This is an old campfire favorite, long ago used by cowboys on the open range and still enjoyed today in kitchens with central heat and air. To this very day, Trail Blazin' Beef Soup welcomes a cold, wet hunter like a mother's hug.

MAKES 6 TO 8 SERVINGS

6 tablespoons olive oil

2 pounds chuck pot roast, trimmed and cut in 1-inch cubes

2 cloves garlic, minced

2 teaspoons ground cumin

3 cups coarsely chopped white onions

5 cups beef stock (see p. 43)

3 cups water

9 red potatoes, scrubbed and halved

3 cups kernel corn, frozen or fresh

3 carrots, peeled and cut in 1-inch chunks

2 medium zucchinis, cut in 1-inch pieces

1/2 cup coarsely chopped cilantro

1 teaspoon salt

1/2 teaspoon pepper

flour tortillas, on the side

Heat 3 tablespoons of the olive oil in a large skillet. Stir-fry the meat, garlic, and cumin for 2 to 3 minutes. Remove with a slotted spoon to a 6- to 8-quart stockpot.

Add the onions to the skillet with the remaining 3 tablespoons of olive oil and sauté until soft. This usually takes 2 to 3 minutes. Remove to the stockpot.

Add all the remaining ingredients to the stockpot, and bring to a boil. Cover, reduce heat and simmer 1 hour or longer.

Serve with flour tortillas.

Cream Corn Soup

When the corn stalks first start showing their little ol' ears, my mind wanders in the direction of my mother's Cream Corn Soup. Here's that very recipe. Fresh corn makes a huge difference.

MAKES 4 TO 6 SERVINGS

2 tablespoons butter

1 cup chopped white onions

2½ cups fresh or frozen corn

¼ cup chopped canned pimento

4 cups chicken stock (see p. 44)

1 teaspoon salt

1 teaspoon black pepper

½ cup heavy cream

paprika for garnish

In a saucepan, melt the butter over medium heat and sauté the onions for 1 minute, until soft and translucent, but not browned. Be careful, as butter scorches easily. Use low heat if necessary, and stir constantly to avoid scorching. Turn the heat down to low, if you haven't already, and add the corn. Cook uncovered about 10 minutes, stirring every 2 minutes or so to avoid scorching and sticking. Set aside to cool.

When the corn is cool, place it in a blender with pimento and 1 cup of the chicken broth. Blend to puree consistency.

Place the remaining 3 cups of broth in a saucepan and bring it to a boil, adding salt and pepper to taste. Lower the heat and add the corn puree, simmering uncovered for 10 minutes.

Thoroughly mix in the cream, cover, and turn the heat off. Let the soup stand covered for a couple of minutes so the cream can warm.

Serve the soup immediately in small bowls, garnishing with a sprinkle of paprika.

South Texas Chili

I call the next three recipes my Tri-State Chili Trilogy. You might want to try all three before you decide which one you want to hunker down with on a cold day.

Each variation brings home the essence of this non-traditional approach to chili-making. South Texas Chili should bring back fond memories to anyone who's ever ducked into a greasy spoon in the lower Rio Grande Valley of Texas, with one noticeable exception: Using turkey instead of ground beef might add a day or two to your life.

The green chiles can be found at most grocery stores. One 4-ounce can equals 4 tablespoons. If you can't find the green chiles, use green or red bell peppers.

Chipotle peppers can be found in 7-ounce cans in the Mexican markets. If you prefer spicier chili, use more than 2 peppers. Also, the Chipotle Paste recipe (see p. 124) can be substituted, to taste.

MAKES 4 TO 6 SERVINGS

1 pound ground turkey

1 tablespoon oil or bacon drippings

1 tablespoon chili powder

1 1/2 teaspoons cumin

2 cloves garlic, sliced

1/2 teaspoon salt

1/2 teaspoon black pepper

1 tablespoon cornstarch

1/2 teaspoon dried leaf oregano

4 tablespoons coarsely chopped white onions

4 tablespoons coarsely chopped green chiles

2 whole chipotle peppers in adobo sauce

1 14-ounce can chopped tomatoes

1 cup chicken stock (see p. 44)

Using a black cast-iron skillet, brown the turkey for 2 1/2 to 3 minutes in the oil. Add all ingredients except the chipotle peppers, tomatoes, and chicken stock, and sauté for 2 to 3 minutes.

Add the remaining ingredients and cook on high heat for approximately 3 to 5 minutes, then let simmer 4 to 5 minutes.

Adjust salt and pepper to taste, and serve immediately.

SERVING SUGGESTION
These chili dishes are excellent served over steamed rice or noodles.

New Mexico Chili

The second part of my Tri-State Chili Trilogy is a doff of the hat to my neighbors to the west. Notice that all three of these recipes can be knocked off in less than 15 minutes—if you put your mind to it.

MAKES 4 TO 6 SERVINGS

1 pound ground pork (or turkey)

1 tablespoon oil or bacon drippings

1 tablespoon chili powder

$\frac{1}{2}$ teaspoon cumin

2 garlic cloves, sliced

$\frac{1}{2}$ teaspoon salt

$\frac{1}{2}$ teaspoon black pepper

1 tablespoon cornstarch

$1\frac{1}{2}$ teaspoons dried leaf oregano

4 tablespoons coarsely chopped white onions

4 tablespoons coarsely chopped green chiles

2 whole chipotle peppers in adobo sauce

1 14-ounce can chopped tomatoes

1 cup chicken stock (see p. 44)

1 14-ounce can white hominy

Using a black cast-iron skillet, brown the pork for $2\frac{1}{2}$ to 3 minutes in the oil. Add all ingredients except the chipotle peppers, tomatoes, chicken stock, and hominy. Sauté for 2 to 3 minutes.

Add the remaining ingredients and cook on high heat for approximately 3 to 5 minutes, then let simmer 4 to 5 minutes. Adjust salt and pepper to taste, and serve immediately.

COOKING SUGGESTION
Corn may also be substituted for the hominy.

Cajun Chili

I'm not about to recommend to a Cajun how to doctor up a bowl of anything, whether it's gumbo, chili, or whatever. But try this simple method first, before soaking it in Tabasco or some other hot sauce. You might be surprised how nicely it stands on its own.

MAKES 4 TO 6 SERVINGS

1 pound ground turkey (or pork)

1 tablespoon oil or bacon drippings

1 tablespoon chili powder

1½ teaspoons cumin

2 garlic cloves, sliced

½ teaspoon salt

½ teaspoon black pepper

1 tablespoon cornstarch

½ teaspoon dried leaf oregano

1 bay leaf

4 tablespoons coarsely chopped white onions

4 tablespoons green chiles

2 coarsely chopped chipotle peppers in adobo sauce

1 14-ounce can chopped tomatoes

1 cup chicken stock (see p. 44)

2 cups (or 1 14-ounce can) kidney beans

Using a black cast-iron skillet, brown the turkey for 2½ to 3 minutes in the oil. Add all ingredients except the chipotle peppers, tomatoes, chicken stock, and kidney beans. Sauté for 2 to 3 minutes.

Add the remaining ingredients and cook on high heat for approximately 5 to 10 minutes, then let simmer 4 to 5 minutes. Remove the bay leaf, adjust salt and pepper to taste, and serve immediately.

SERVING SUGGESTION
Serve over steamed rice or noodles. Corn may be substituted for the kidney beans.

Matt's Big-Time Eatin' Turkey Chili

No one will ever know it's not beef—unless you break down and tell 'em yourself.

MAKES 4 TO 6 SERVINGS

1 pound ground turkey

1 tablespoon cooking oil of your choice

1 tablespoon chili powder

1½ tablespoons cumin

1 large clove garlic, sliced

½ tablespoon salt

½ tablespoon black pepper

1 tablespoon cornstarch

½ tablespoon dried leaf oregano

4 tablespoons coarsely chopped sweet white onions

4 tablespoons coarsely chopped New Mexico-style green chiles

1 14-ounce can whole stewed tomatoes

2 whole chipotle peppers in adobo sauce

1 cup chicken stock (see p. 44)

Preferably using a black cast-iron skillet, brown the turkey in the oil for 2½ to 3 minutes.

Add all the ingredients except the tomatoes, chipotle peppers, and chicken stock, and sauté for 2 to 3 minutes.

Add the remaining ingredients and cook for approximately 5 to 10 minutes.

Adjust seasoning to taste. Serve immediately.

Matt's Pork Chili

On my way to New Mexico, I came across an old crock pot at a garage sale. It was beat up, but I pulled the sleeve out of the pot and started cooking all my gumbos, beans, and chilis out of it.

That old pot holds up over an open fire, electric, gas, or coals. It hasn't broken on me yet. These days when I go to garage sales, I look for more beat-up crock pots.

This particular chili is a Texas special with a New Mexican twist. I first made it out in the woods, where things always taste better.

MAKES 4 TO 6 SERVINGS

1 pound ground or cubed pork

1 tablespoon chili powder

1½ tablespoons cumin

1 large clove garlic, sliced

½ tablespoon salt

½ tablespoon black pepper

1 tablespoon cornstarch

½ tablespoon dried leaf oregano

4 tablespoons coarsely chopped sweet white onions

4 tablespoons coarsely chopped New Mexico-style green chiles

1 14-ounce can whole stewed tomatoes

2 whole chipotle peppers in adobo sauce

1 cup chicken stock (see p. 44)

In a moderately hot skillet (preferably black cast-iron) or crock pot, cook the pork for 3 to 4 minutes.

Add all the ingredients except the tomatoes, chipotle peppers, and chicken stock. Sauté for 2 to 3 minutes.

Add the remaining ingredients and cook at very low heat for 15 minutes.

Adjust seasoning to taste, and serve immediately.

Matt's Big-Time Eatin' Turkey Chili with Veggies

You'll impress your guests more if you can use wild turkey instead of store-bought. Wild turkey has more flavor.

Any kind of root vegetables will do (broccoli, squash, zucchini, cauliflower, carrots). Don't let them get mushy on you; they're best with some body and firmness.

MAKES 4 TO 6 SERVINGS

1 pound ground turkey

1¹/₂ tablespoons cooking oil

1 tablespoon paprika

³/₄ tablespoon cumin

2 large cloves garlic, sliced

³/₄ tablespoon salt

³/₄ tablespoon black pepper

1¹/₂ tablespoons cornstarch

³/₄ tablespoon dried leaf oregano

4 tablespoons coarsely chopped sweet white onions

4 tablespoons coarsely chopped New Mexico-style green chiles

1 14-ounce can whole stewed tomatoes

2 whole chipotle peppers in adobo sauce

1 cup fresh or frozen corn

1 cup finely chopped zucchini

1 cup chicken stock (see p. 44)

Preferably using a black cast-iron skillet, brown the turkey in the oil for 2¹/₂ to 3 minutes.

Add all the ingredients except the vegetables and chicken stock, and sauté for 2 to 3 minutes.

Add the vegetables and stock, and cook for approximately 5 to 10 minutes.

Adjust seasoning to taste, and serve immediately.

Texas Campfire Chili

Some things simply fit, kind of like a farmer and his seed. My friends at the Texas Beef Council know a thing or two about campfires and starry nights and chili.

Sometimes there's a tendency for folks to get a little too cute with their chili, which is why we see so many variations. This one is simple and to the point. Many good things in life are.

MAKES 4 TO 6 SERVINGS

1¹/₂ pounds trimmed chuck cut in ¹/₂-inch cubes

1 large coarsely chopped white onion (reserve some for garnish)

1 clove garlic, minced

2 cups spicy tomato juice

1 15-ounce can Hunt's chopped tomatoes

1 cup beef stock (see p. 43)

2 tablespoons chili powder

¹/₂ teaspoon salt

¹/₄ teaspoon pepper

¹/₄ teaspoon cayenne pepper

2 teaspoons cumin powder

1 teaspoon oregano

1 tablespoon masa corn flour

1 tablespoon water

shredded Cheddar cheese as a garnish

Brown the meat and onion in a pot, and drain off the excess fat. Add the remaining ingredients except the masa and water.

Simmer over low heat for 2 hours, adding more water if needed.

Combine the masa with the water, and whisk it until smooth. Add the masa to the bubbling chili, and continue cooking for 15 minutes or until thickened.

SERVING SUGGESTION
Top your chili with cheese and more onions, and grab the crackers.

Beef and Black Bean Chili

This is my spin on a Texas Beef Council favorite. I've never been a real fan of black beans, but they do look pretty in chili. If you've got my taste buds, substitute navy or pinto beans.

MAKES 6 SERVINGS

3 cups (or a 15-ounce can) dried black beans

4 cups water

2 pounds round steak

3 tablespoons olive oil

2 coarsely chopped large bell peppers

1 coarsely chopped large white onion

2 chopped jalapeños, seeded

3 cloves garlic, crushed

½ cup chili powder

1 tablespoon ground cumin

1 teaspoon salt

½ teaspoon black pepper

1 28-ounce can crushed tomatoes

1 cup shredded sharp Cheddar cheese

¾ cup sour cream

sourdough bread

Cover the beans in cold water and soak them for 12 hours or overnight. Drain and rinse the beans.

Bring the beans to a boil in 4 cups of water in a large saucepan, and then reduce the heat. Cover the beans tightly and simmer 1 to 1¼ hours, or until beans are tender.

Trim the excess fat from the beef, and cut the beef into half-inch cubes.

Heat the olive oil in a Dutch oven over medium heat. Add the bell peppers, onion, jalapeños, and garlic. Cook for 10 minutes or until tender, stirring frequently.

Increase the heat to high, and add the beef. Cook for 6 minutes or until the beef is no longer pink, stirring frequently.

Reduce the heat to low and stir in the chili powder, cumin, salt, and pepper. Continue to stir for 1 minute, then stir in the beans and tomatoes.

Cover and simmer 1 hour and 20 minutes. Add more water if needed.

Transfer the chili to serving bowls. Serve with cheese, sour cream, and sourdough bread.

Beef Stew with Homemade Dumplings

Here's a real stick-to-your-ribs entree. You won't find anyone who does them like this.

Warning: Eating the following stew may cause drowsiness, so don't be operating any heavy machinery or driving on a bellyful.

Thanks to my friends at the Texas Beef Council for the basic recipe.

MAKES 4 SERVINGS

1/4 cup flour

1 teaspoon dried thyme

1/2 teaspoon pepper

1/2 teaspoon salt

1 pound beef round steak, cubed

2 tablespoons oil

1 bay leaf

3 cups beef stock (see p. 43)

1/4 cup red wine

1/2 pound carrots in 1-inch chunks

2 cups large onion in 1-inch chunks

4 cups medium potatoes in 1-inch chunks

1 stalk celery in 1-inch chunks

fresh parsley (for garnish)

DUMPLINGS

2 cups biscuit mix

2/3 cup milk

Thoroughly mix the flour, thyme, pepper, and salt, then coat the beef cubes in the dry mixture.

In a Dutch oven, sauté the beef in oil over low to moderate heat until the cubes are browned on all sides.

Add the bay leaf, beef broth, and wine to the beef cubes. Bring to a boil, then reduce the heat and cover and simmer for 1 hour, or until the beef is tender. Stir occasionally.

Add the carrots, onions, potatoes, and celery to the stew and bring to a boil, then reduce the heat and cover and simmer for 40 minutes.

Uncover the stew, remove the bay leaf, and drop the dumpling mixture by the tablespoonfuls into the boiling stew. Cook the dumplings 10 minutes uncovered over low heat.

Cover the stew, and cook the dumplings 10 minutes longer. If desired, sprinkle the stew with chopped parsley.

New Mexican Jalapeño Stew with Pork

My good friends Virginia and Larry Wright and I worked on this recipe under the big stars at Mesa Redondo, out of Tucumcari, New Mexico.

The New Mexican recipes in this book were proofed on their ranch and influenced by their opinions, along with some 80-proof whiskey and a dipping spoon.

MAKES 8 TO 10 SERVINGS

2 tablespoons oil of your choice or bacon drippings

3 pounds cubed pork (I prefer pork shoulder)

1 cup diced white onions

2 4-ounce cans diced green chiles

2 20-ounce cans whole tomatoes, chopped

1½ teaspoons kosher salt

2 cups water

1 teaspoon oregano

2 cloves garlic, thinly sliced

1 bay leaf (optional)

4 tablespoons thinly sliced fresh jalapeños

¼ cup vinegar or to taste

Preheat the oil or bacon drippings on moderate heat in your favorite cooking pot, and cook the pork and onions until the pork is lightly brown, about 5 to 10 minutes.

Add the green chiles, tomatoes, salt, water, oregano, garlic, and bay leaf, and simmer on low heat.

In a bowl, combine the jalapeños and vinegar. Let the jalapeños sit for 30 minutes, then discard the vinegar. While the stew is simmering, add half of the jalapeños.

Continue simmering for 30 minutes. Taste for spiciness. If you want more heat, add as many jalapeños as your little heart desires.

Total cooking time is 2 hours, or until the pork is tender. Remove the bay leaf before serving.

Shrimp Stew

My three favorite hangover cures are Menudo (see p. 42), Oyster Stew, and this Shrimp Stew. I've had it many mornings, and I'm here to testify: Shrimp Stew with plenty of good Chipotle Paste (see p. 124) or hot sauce on the side will run the poison right out of your system.

I actually like it best in the wee hours, after a night out of hollering and screaming and throwing rocks with the troops.

At a glance, this recipe looks like a major pain in the ol' bee-hind, but it's not. The little extra work is well worth the trouble.

MAKES 4 TO 6 SERVINGS

1 pound medium shrimp with shells

4 tablespoons butter

1 cup chicken stock (see p. 44)

1 tablespoon flour

$^1/_2$ teaspoon salt

$^1/_4$ teaspoon white pepper

$^1/_4$ cup coarsely chopped white onions

2 tablespoons finely chopped celery

1 clove garlic, finely chopped

2 cups milk

1 cup half-and-half

2 tablespoons chopped parsley, as a garnish

Peel the shrimp, and place the shells in a small skillet or saucepan with 2 tablespoons of butter. Sauté on moderate heat for 3 to 4 minutes.

Add the chicken stock, and simmer on low for 5 to 8 minutes.

While the shells are simmering in the saucepan, add the remaining 2 tablespoons of butter, flour, salt, pepper, onions, celery, and garlic to a skillet. Cook on low for 2 to 3 minutes, being careful not to brown the flour.

Add the shrimp, and cook 2 to 3 minutes more, frequently stirring and turning the shrimp.

To the shells, add the milk and half-and-half, and bring to a boil.

Strain the shelled mixture into the skillet with the shrimp, and cook an additional 2 to 3 minutes on low heat. Serve in warm bowls, garnishing with the chopped parsley.

Rabbit Stew

I was a young lad the first time I ever harvested a bunny. We were living in South Austin on Jewell Street, and I was the proud owner of a pellet gun.

One day I wandered down by the creek and spotted a furry animal, which I figured to be a cat. When I saw it was a wild rabbit, my heart went to my throat.

I couldn't have been more excited if it had been a tiger or lion. I was feeling pretty good on the way home, but when I saw my Granny Gaytan's eyes light up at the sight of me and that rabbit, I could have done a backward somersault right there I was so proud.

This recipe also works great with chicken thighs and legs, in quarters.

MAKES 4 SERVINGS

1 cup oil (not olive)

1 teaspoon salt

1 teaspoon black pepper

2 pounds rabbit or chicken cut into serving pieces

flour for dusting

1 cup finely chopped white onions

2 cloves mashed fresh garlic

1/2 cup diced potatoes

1/2 cup diced carrots

2 cups water

1 bay leaf

1 cup chopped fresh tomatoes

1 cup white wine

1 tablespoon vinegar

Heat the oil in a large skillet over medium heat. Meanwhile, salt and pepper the rabbit pieces, and roll each piece in the flour.

When the oil is hot but not smoking, add the rabbit pieces and fry over medium heat for 5 to 7 minutes, until well-browned. Occasionally stir the pieces around to assure an even browning.

Once browned, set aside the meat in a separate dish. Drain off all but 1 teaspoon of the oil from the frying pan. Scrape the bottom of the skillet with a metal spoon to loosen up any stuck bits of meat and browned flour, but do not remove.

Add the onions, garlic, potatoes, and carrots to the skillet, and sauté 1 minute over medium heat, stirring constantly to avoid scorching, until the onion is soft and translucent but not browned.

Return the meat, and add 2 cups of water, the bay leaf, tomatoes, white wine, and vinegar. Cook covered for 45 minutes to 1 hour, or until the meat is tender and about to fall off the bone.

If the stew starts to dry out, add 1 to 2 teaspoons of broth, as necessary. Remove the bay leaf and serve while hot.

SERVING SUGGESTION
Serve Rabbit Stew with your favorite vegetable salad. *Frijoles a la charra* also go well with this dish. Corn tortillas or good French bread can be used for sopping up the last bit of gravy.

Gumbo Roux

I don't want to insult any Cajuns or Louisianans, but there are almost as many ways to make a roux as to make a gumbo. I mix grease and flour because I don't like to use water.

I'll grant you, the key to any gumbo is the roux; but, a good roux is not as complicated as some think.

Gumbo should be a labor of love, and this roux gets you headed down Lovers' Lane. It's very basic and down-home. You can get fancy and modify it later if you wish. But first it's best to get the basics down.

ROUX FOR 6 TO 8 SERVINGS

½ cup vegetable oil (or lard, bacon drippings, butter, or any combination thereof)

½ cup flour

OVEN METHOD

Preheat your oven to 400°.

Add the oil to a 10-inch cast-iron skillet, and place the skillet into the heated oven. When the oil is hot, remove the skillet from the oven and thoroughly mix in the flour.

Return the skillet to the oven.

Take great care not to burn the roux, stirring every 15 minutes. After 15 minutes, the roux will be blond. In 30 minutes, the roux will be light brown. In 45 minutes the roux will be light chocolate. In 1 hour the roux will be dark chocolate.

STOVETOP METHOD

Heat the oil in a 10-inch cast-iron skillet to hot. Reduce the heat to low and thoroughly mix in the flour. At this time, serve yourself a nice glass of red wine or your favorite beverage. Crank up your favorite music (something with a Cajun accordion, if handy) and gently stir the roux with a flat-edged spatula, which allows you to gently skim and caress the roux. Halfway through your beverage, the roux will be blond.

After one beverage the roux will be light brown.

At the start of your second beverage, the roux will be light chocolate.

After two beverages, the roux will be dark chocolate.

Game Hen Gumbo

The following gumbo recipes are not very busy. Feel free to throw in other ingredients. I've had good luck with hominy, black beans, corn, carrots, and peas. Another good thing about gumbo is that the meat and vegetable ingredients are not all that exact. No two gumbos are ever alike.

Game hens are tender by nature. Don't let them fall apart in the gumbo, or you'll have a bony mess.

MAKES 6 SERVINGS

1 batch of roux

3-4 cloves garlic, thinly sliced

1 teaspoon black pepper

1 teaspoon salt

1/2 teaspoon white pepper

1/2 teaspoon thyme

1 1/2 cups coarsely chopped white onions

3/4 cup coarsely chopped celery

3/4 cup coarsely chopped red or green bell peppers

2 cups sliced okra, fresh or frozen

3 whole fresh jalapeños

6 cups chicken stock (see p. 44)

1 15-ounce can chopped tomatoes

4 game hens

flour for dusting

6 ounces portabello mushrooms, cubed

1 bay leaf

Prepare the roux (see p. 34).

Add all the spices except the bay leaf to the roux. Also add all the vegetables except the tomatoes, and cook over moderate heat for 3 to 4 minutes.

Add the stock and tomatoes. Bring to a boil, then turn the heat to low, simmering very gently for 1 1/2 hours.

Split the game hens in half and dust them with flour.

Cover the bottom of a separate skillet with approximately 1/4-inch of oil, and sauté the game hens until they are golden brown. Once the game hens are golden brown, add them to the gumbo.

Add the mushrooms to the same skillet where the game hens were browned, and sauté them until they are soft.

Add the sautéed mushrooms and the bay leaf to the gumbo, and cook for 20 to 30 minutes, taking care not to allow the game hens to fall apart. Remove the bay leaf and serve over the rice of your choice.

Dove & Sausage Gumbo

The flavors in this gumbo will make your tongue do a slow waltz one minute and a cha-cha the next. It doesn't even take two to tango if you make it right, but it never hurts to have a partner in the same room.

MAKES 6 SERVINGS

1 batch of roux

3-4 cloves garlic, thinly sliced

1 teaspoon black pepper

1 teaspoon salt

1/2 teaspoon white pepper

1/2 teaspoon thyme

1 1/2 cups coarsely chopped white onions

3/4 cup coarsely chopped celery

3/4 cup coarsely chopped bell peppers

2 cups sliced okra, fresh or frozen

3 whole fresh jalapeños

6 cups chicken stock (see p. 44)

1 15-ounce can chopped tomatoes

1 pound your favorite smoked sausage

2 cups (approximately 1 pound) dove breast

1 bay leaf

Prepare the roux (see p. 34).

Add all the spices except the bay leaf and all the vegetables except the canned tomatoes. Cook over moderate heat for 3 to 4 minutes.

Add the stock and tomatoes, and bring to a boil, then turn the heat down to low. Simmer very gently for 1 1/2 hours.

Pour 1/4 cup of water in a separate skillet, add the sausage, and let it simmer until lightly brown.

Add the dove breast to the skillet, and toss the dove and sausage together, continuing to simmer for 3 to 5 more minutes.

Add the sausage and dove mixture and the bay leaf to the gumbo and cook 1 hour more or until dove is tender. Remove the bay leaf before serving.

Matt's Favorite Gumbo

The drumsticks and gizzards in this gumbo should still be firm at eating time. Don't let the drumsticks fall off the bones.

MAKES 6 SERVINGS

1 batch of roux

1 pound chicken gizzards

3-4 cloves garlic, thinly sliced

1 teaspoon black pepper

1 teaspoon salt

$^1/_2$ teaspoon white pepper

$^1/_2$ teaspoon thyme

1$^1/_2$ cups coarsely chopped white onions

$^3/_4$ cup coarsely chopped celery

$^3/_4$ cup coarsely chopped bell peppers

2 cups sliced okra, fresh or frozen

3 whole fresh jalapeños

6 cups chicken stock (see p. 44)

1 15-ounce can chopped tomatoes

6 to 8 chicken drumsticks

2 cups fresh or frozen corn

2 cups diced zucchini or summer squash

1 bay leaf

Prepare the roux (see p. 34).

Thoroughly rinse the gizzards.

To the roux, add all the spices except the bay leaf and all the vegetables except the canned tomatoes, corn, and zucchini, and continue cooking over moderate heat for 3 to 4 minutes.

Add the stock and tomatoes. Bring to a boil, and then turn down the heat to low, simmering very gently for 1$^1/_2$ hours.

Cover the bottom of a separate skillet with approximately $^1/_2$ -inch of oil, and sauté the drumsticks until they are golden brown. Add the golden legs and gizzards to the gumbo, and gently cook for 1 hour.

Add the corn, zucchini (or squash), and the bay leaf to the gumbo, and gently simmer for 30 minutes.

Seafood Gumbo

When I think about Cajun food, alligators crawl through the bayous of my mind. If I were just a little bit braver, I'd toss some gator into one of these gumbos. Alligators are excellent fried, stewed, or gumboed, but I'm getting queasy just mentioning the rascals.

That's because my friend Tommy Granbury and I went on the first legalized alligator hunt ever sanctioned by the Texas Parks & Wildlife Department. A couple of wardens came along to make sure we followed all the rules; and, Russell Tinsley, the outdoor writer for the Austin American-Statesman, also tagged along with a black-and-white camera because he said he wanted to document the day Tommy and I got eaten.

The wardens informed us we could catch gators by one of two methods: (1) with a snare; or (2) with a big, baited hook.

Tommy and I chose the bait method because catching an alligator on a snare and dragging it on land to kill it sounded a tad hazardous.

When we arrived on the bayous outside of Houston, we embraced a beautiful early evening that included a pink sunset. Tommy and I felt fairly confident as we baited nine heavy lines with big ol' fat yellow chickens. These weren't Caspers—the white-with-no-fat kind you see advertised at a supermarket near you; they were yellow and plump.

The law says once you put out a line, you have to run it. You've got to check it on occasion to make sure no animal is suffering on it, and you've got to take it up when you're through. We were to begin checking the lines early the next morning.

Everything was working beautifully until it started raining. And raining. And raining.

By the next morning, the water level had crept several inches over the door handles of Russell Tinsley's automobile.

We knew where our lines were, but they were now three or four feet underwater. The wardens said we had to run them anyway.

"It might be a little dangerous running them underwater," I suggested. "What if there's a big ol' alligator down there waiting on us?"

One warden nodded and said, "I don't believe we would have done it this way, but the law says you've got to run these lines."

I grabbed a long pole, and Tommy and I each pulled a pistol and waded out into three feet of murky swamp. We were quite thrilled that the first six lines came up empty.

The key to this hunt was getting out alive. Mounds and mounds of red ants kept floating by, and Tommy and I must have had 80 to 100 bites apiece all over our bodies.

Then we got to Number 7 and forgot about the bites. When we tugged on the line, it tugged back. We tugged again, and it tugged back some more.

I looked about 15 yards into the water and spotted two of the beadiest eyes you ever care to see staring right back at us.

Suddenly, the water exploded as the gator flapped his tail and blew right between us. Tommy and I jumped straight up at the same time, like a couple of fat mud hens trying to clear water.

You know that nightmare we all have when you open your mouth and nothing comes out? Tommy and I did not make a peep, but our mouths were wide open.

Fortunately, the alligator blew right up on the ground and tangled himself in some heavy bushes. He sort of caught himself. Thank goodness and thank God.

"You boys still have a couple more lines to go, don't you?" one of the wardens asked.

"Oh, surely no more than one," I lied.

Durned if something didn't tug back on the eighth line, too, but this time Tommy and I turned white before anything happened.

We were lucky hunters again. This gator had rolled and wrapped around in the line so much, we were able to drag him to shore, steering clear of the head and tail.

"That oughta 'bout do it," Tommy announced.

"Naw, you got another to go," the warden said. Tommy and I were getting very tired of his voice by now.

We called a timeout and I pulled out my old buddy Jack Daniel's for help with that last line. Luckily, it was emptier than that bottle of Jack once all was said and done.

Tommy and I still have the hides and heads of those gators. The meat went quick—fried, stewed, and gumboed.

Today, whenever someone asks me if I'd like to go alligator hunting, I give them the ol' "been-there, done-that" pitch. I don't even want to see one floating around in a pot. That's why I stick to this Seafood Gumbo.

MAKES 6 SERVINGS

1 batch of roux

3-4 cloves garlic, thinly sliced

1 teaspoon black pepper

1 teaspoon salt

½ teaspoon white pepper

½ teaspoon thyme

1½ cups coarsely chopped white onions

¾ cup coarsely chopped celery

¾ cup coarsely chopped bell peppers

2 cups sliced okra, fresh or frozen

3 whole fresh jalapeños

6 cups fish stock

1 15-ounce can chopped tomatoes

½ pound breakfast sausage, cooked, crumbled, and drained

1 bay leaf

1 pound raw peeled shrimp

½ pound crab meat, imitation or real

1 pint oysters

Prepare the roux (see p. 34).

Add all the spices except the bay leaf and all the vegetables except the canned tomatoes, cooking for 3 to 4 minutes over moderate heat.

Add the stock and tomatoes. Bring to a boil, and then turn down the heat to low, simmering very gently for 1½ to 2 hours.

Add the sausage and the bay leaf to the gumbo and cook 1 hour.

Ten minutes before serving, add the shrimp.

Five minutes after adding the shrimp, add the crab and oysters. Cook very gently. Remove the bay leaf before serving.

SERVING SUGGESTION
This gumbo is great over rice.

The Real Breakfast
of Champions
(Menudo Tripe Soup)

Just in case you're inclined to suffer hangovers, here's a recipe good to cure six to eight of them, straight from your friendly Dr. Matt. And yes, Dr. Matt does make housecalls—once you've perfected this soup.

MAKES 6 TO 8 SERVINGS

3$^1/_2$ to 4 pounds beef tripe

2 quarts water

1 tablespoon salt

2 pigs feet, split and washed

6 cloves garlic, minced

2$^1/_2$ cups coarsely chopped sweet white onions

1$^1/_2$ tablespoons crushed Mexican oregano

2 tablespoons chili powder

2 15-ounce cans hominy

Wash the tripe in cold water and drain.

Trim the fat and cut the tripe into 1-inch cubes, or smaller. Rinse the tripe again.

Bring the tripe to a boil in a large stockpot with water and salt, then simmer it on low to medium heat for 1 hour, skimming as needed.

Add all the other ingredients and simmer for 1$^1/_2$ to 2 hours, or until the tripe is tender.

Add water or beef broth (optional) as needed to keep the pot at its original liquid level.

The Best Beef Stock

I want to give you three stocks, or broths, that work great in all kinds of soups.

4 to 4¹/₂ pounds beef (¹/₂ short ribs and ¹/₂ beef necks or soup bones with lots of meat)

4 quarts water

2 teaspoons salt

1 teaspoon black pepper

2 cups coarsely chopped sweet white onions

³/₄ cup coarsely chopped celery

1 cup coarsely chopped and peeled carrots

6 cloves garlic, crushed and coarsely chopped

1 bay leaf

In a large stockpot, combine the beef, water, salt, and pepper. Bring to a boil and simmer gently 1¹/₂ hours, skimming as needed.

Add all other ingredients, and simmer another 1¹/₂ hours.

Strain through a cheesecloth and refrigerate.

This will keep in a refrigerator 2 to 3 days. You can also store in 1-cup Ziploc bags in the freezer.

New & Improved Mild Turkey Stock

If you prefer chicken stock, simply replace the turkey parts with chicken parts.

4 to 4½ pounds turkey parts
(I recommend wings and
necks)

4 quarts water

2 teaspoons salt

1 teaspoon black pepper

2 cups coarsely chopped sweet
white onions

¾ cup coarsely chopped celery

1 cup coarsely chopped and
peeled carrots

4 cloves garlic, crushed and
coarsely chopped

1 bay leaf

Wash and disjoint the turkey wings.

In a large stockpot, combine the wings, necks, water, salt, and pepper. Bring to a boil and simmer gently 1½ hours, skimming as needed.

Add all other ingredients and simmer another 1½ hours.

Strain through a cheesecloth and refrigerate.

This will keep in a refrigerator 2 to 3 days. You can also store in 1-cup Ziploc bags in the freezer.

COOKING SUGGESTION
Use to lace soups, rice, beans, and mashed potatoes.

Boiled Shrimp and Shrimp Stock
(2 Birds, 1 Stone)

Boil up some shrimp and make yourself some shrimp stock, as well.

MAKES 1 CUP OF STOCK

1 pound headless, shell-on, raw
   shrimp

3 cups water

2 tablespoons lemon juice

$^1/_2$ teaspoon salt

4 peppercorns

1 cup coarsely chopped white
   onions

$^1/_2$ cup coarsely chopped celery

1 clove garlic, thinly sliced

$^1/_2$ bay leaf

1 jalapeño sliced in half

Peel the shrimp and reserve the shells.

In a stockpot, place all the ingredients except the shrimp, but do include the shells. Bring to a boil and simmer very gently for 30 minutes.

Strain after 30 minutes, removing all solid particles.

Return the broth back into the stockpot and bring to a boil.

Add the shrimp and cover. Cook 3 to 5 minutes, depending on the size of the shrimp. When the shrimp is pretty and pink, strain.

Place the boiled shrimp in a Ziploc bag, and place the bag in an ice bath (ice and water) to stop the shrimp cooking process.

Reduce the stock to 1 cup and reserve for shrimp or seafood sauces or to spice up rice or chowder.

When the boiled shrimp has cooled, eat it as a cocktail or in a salad.

CHAPTER THREE
Side Dishes

IF YOU'VE DONE YOUR SHARE OF COOKING for others, you've already been in situations where the side dish has carried the entire meal. Even the top dogs sometimes mess up on the main event, but a side dish can come through like a champ and save the day. That's why I like to prepare several sides, just to make sure *somebody's* happy.

One really good side can raise the quality of an average entree. Don't neglect your sides.

Whole Pinto Beans

I once knew this gentleman so devastated by his mother's passing that he delayed going through her possessions for ten years. One day he finally collected himself and decided to take a peek at a few things still stored in her garage. Near one dark corner, he spotted a big gallon jar of dried pinto beans. The jar jogged his memory, sending him back to those days when, as a young boy, he watched from the kitchen floor while his mom cooked beans on an old gas range. He looked inside the jar and figured if he scooped out one cup a year, he had enough beans to last a decade.

Every Christmas, he measured the beans in his mom's porcelain coffee cup, soaked and cooked them, and ate them alone, while reminiscing about dear ol' mom. He went through maybe six cups before joining her in the Great Beyond. On the day he died, Mom must have had a pot waiting because the heavens were laced with the fragrance of her pintos.

Back in the old days, a cowboy might carry dried beans around in his saddlebags for several years. Soaking was much more of a necessity back then. Today's beans do not require so much attention.

I've never been big on soaking beans, but for those who must soak for sentimental reasons, I understand completely.

MAKES 6 TO 8 SERVINGS

2 cups (1 pound) pinto beans

6 cups water

1/2 pound salt pork

1/2 cup finely chopped white onions

1 clove garlic, crushed

1 big, plump, ripe tomato, chopped

1/2 bay leaf

In a large pot, bring the beans and water to a boil. Cover the pot and simmer the beans over low heat for 1 hour.

In a skillet, chop the salt pork into little cubes and sauté. Add the onions, garlic, and tomato to the skillet. Simmer the pork and vegetable mixture until everything is cooked.

Add the mixture and the bay leaf to the bean pot, and simmer for 1 1/2 to 2 hours, until the beans are tender. You will need to continually add water to the pot, so the beans do not dry up. Remove the bay leaf before serving.

48 • SIDE DISHES

Ranch Style Pinto Beans

In Texas, the pinto is the queen of beans. Pintos are nutritious and have many pals. Pintos enjoy hanging out with sausages, bacon, meats (both wild and domestic), onions, garlic, tortillas—durn near anything.

Good beans swim equally well in water or broth (beef, chicken, pork, or veggie). Beans can be heated and reheated, fried and refried. They can be scooped, spread, mashed, or chucked across the room. They can be cooked over many fires—wood, gas, buffalo chips. They can be crocked over a pit, or "Edisoned" on a countertop crock pot, pressure-cooked, baked, or boiled. Beans are long-lasting in more ways than one. (Nothing like beans can clean out a room, car, tent, or any space where the wind don't blow.) These Ranch Style Pintos are among my favorites.

MAKES 6 TO 8 SERVINGS

1 cup finely chopped white onions

2 cups coarsely chopped tomatoes

¼ cup lard (no substitutions)

1 tablespoon chili powder

2 cloves garlic, crushed

6 cups water

2 cups (1 pound) pinto beans

1 3-ounce package pork rinds

4 whole jalapeños

In a separate skillet, heat the lard until it is smoking and then back off. Let the lard sit for a while, allowing it to cool down. Carefully add the vegetables, chili powder, and garlic to the hot grease and simmer for 5 to 10 minutes.

In a large pot, add the cooked ingredients, the water, and the beans. Bring the contents of the pot to a boil. Reduce the heat and cook gently for 2½ to 3 hours.

During the last hour of cooking, crumble the pork rinds and add them to the pot.

Leave the 4 jalapeños whole and float them on top of the beans. Simmer until the beans are tender. You will need to continually add water to the pot, so the beans will not dry up.

COOKING SUGGESTION

For spicier beans, crush one jalapeño at a time, and mix it into the beans until the desired heat level is reached.

Fried Peaches No. 2

Sometimes most of your concentration has got to be directed toward your main attraction, which means you don't need to be tangling up your brain on a bunch of difficult side dishes.

Fried Peaches No. 2 (my new and improved fried peaches) is simple, except you're probably going to wish you'd made more. I always do.

3 tablespoons butter

1 tablespoon flour

3 fresh peaches, peeled and
   halved, pit removed

2 tablespoons brown sugar

¼ teaspoon brown cinnamon

⅛ teaspoon (or a pinch)
   cayenne powder

1 ounce peach or apricot
   brandy, or Jack Daniel's

Melt the butter into the flour in a skillet on low heat. Place the peaches cut side down in the buttery flour and cook for 3 to 4 minutes on low heat.

Flip the 6 peach halves over. Mix the sugar, cinnamon, and cayenne together, and sprinkle over the peaches (mostly into the pit holes).

Add the liquor to the butter and flour mix. Cook for 3 to 4 minutes on low heat, basting the peaches for the last minute.

SERVING SUGGESTION
Fried peaches go well with most dishes, especially pork, duck, or wild game.

Fried Hominy

As a small boy, I was invited to eat at a friend's house down the street. His mama fixed up some pork chops and peas and what appeared to be hominy, except I'd never seen hominy without menudo (a Mexican tripe stew known to cure hangovers and many other ills). I looked around for the tripe, but it was simple hominy with black pepper. Made a hominy fan out of me ever since.

MAKES 4 TO 6 SERVINGS

4 slices bacon

3 tablespoons butter

2 cans hominy, white or yellow or 1 of each, drained

salt and pepper to taste

1 tablespoon Parmesan cheese

parsley flakes or green onion, finely chopped, for garnish

Fry the bacon in a skillet until it's crispy. Crumble the bacon on the side.

Reserve 3 tablespoons of bacon drippings in the skillet, adding the butter and hominy over low heat. Cook until the hominy is golden brown (hominy varies, but usually 4 to 5 minutes).

Add salt and pepper to taste. Add the Parmesan cheese and crumbled bacon just before serving.

Garnish with parsley flakes or finely chopped green onions to taste.

Side-Dish Veggie Gumbo

AN OPEN LETTER:

Dear Veggie Friends, Here's a side dish just for you. You know who you are.
Sincerely, Old Meat Breath.

MAKES 4 TO 6 SERVINGS

4 slices bacon

3 tablespoons flour

2 cups coarsely chopped white
   onions

1 cup coarsely chopped green
   bell peppers

1 cup coarsely chopped celery

3 whole jalapeños

2 to 4 cloves garlic, thinly sliced,
   or to taste

2 cups frozen corn
   (or 1 16-ounce can corn)

1 12-ounce can Hunt tomatoes,
   chopped, with juice

1 bay leaf

2 Knorr chicken bouillon cubes

1 cup water

2½ to 3 cups okra, fresh or
   frozen

salt and pepper to taste

Chop up the bacon in 1-inch squares and fry it in a heavy pot until almost crispy. Reserve 3 tablespoons of bacon drippings in the pot (save the rest for other good things). Slightly brown the flour in the drippings on low heat. Add the onions, bell peppers, celery, and jalapeños. Sauté over light to moderate heat until the onions are translucent. Add the garlic and cook 1 minute. Add the corn, tomatoes, bay leaf, bouillon cubes, and cup of water, and cook over moderate heat for 10 to 15 minutes.

Add the okra and cook until tender. Remove the bay leaf and jalapeños, keeping the jalapeños on the side. Adjust the broth with water to taste.

Add salt and pepper to taste.

COOKING SUGGESTION

If you prefer spicy-hot dishes, crunch up the discarded jalapeños and add a little at a time with a spoon until you achieve the spunk you like.

SERVING SUGGESTION

Serve over steamed rice as an excellent side dish for beef, chicken, fish, or any grilled or barbecued main course.

Taste-the-Goodness Beans

This is one of those recipes that makes you realize it doesn't take much to make beans right. The key is to develop a consistency and a rhythm for cooking beans the same way every time.

A bunch of different fancy recipes don't matter; it's what you put in 'em and how long you cook 'em that count. I like to cook mine slower than most, and I use the same bean pot every time.

Taste-the-Goodness Beans are a great, unchallenging side dish because they don't intimidate or offend any main course.

MAKES 6 TO 8 SERVINGS

2 pounds (2 cups) pinto beans

8 cups water

$^{1}/_{2}$ pound salt pork

2 tablespoons flour

In a big pot, cook the beans in water for 1$^{1}/_{2}$ to 2 hours over a light simmer. Adjust the water as needed, making sure the beans are always barely covered.

Cube and lightly brown the salt pork in a skillet over moderate heat. Add the flour to the skillet and let the pork simmer for 2 to 3 minutes.

Add the salt pork and flour to the beans and continue cooking over low heat another 1$^{1}/_{2}$ to 2 hours, adjusting the water as needed. Total cooking time for the beans should be between 3 and 4 hours.

SERVING SUGGESTION

I like to crumble up some cornbread into these beans, along with some finely chopped white onions. Just delicious.

Summer Beans: The Meal

Give me a batch of fluffy biscuits or some cornbread, along with a pretty row of sliced tomatoes and cucumbers covered with a lite vinegar and oil dressing. Then bring on the Summer Beans and stand back.

MAKES 6 TO 8 SERVINGS

2 pounds (2 cups) pinto beans

8 cups water

$1/2$ pound salt pork

3 tablespoons flour

1 cup coarsely chopped white onions

2 cloves garlic, thinly sliced

1 teaspoon dry Mexican oregano flakes

2 cups coarsely chopped zucchini

2 cups corn, fresh or frozen

3 to 4 medium Roma tomatoes, whole

4 beef bouillon cubes (Knorr works best)

salt and pepper to taste

In a big pot, cook the beans in water for $1^1/_2$ to 2 hours over a light simmer. Adjust the water as necessary, making sure the beans are always barely covered.

In a skillet, lightly brown the salt pork, then add the flour, onions, garlic, and oregano, continuing to cook over low heat another 2 to 3 minutes.

Dump what's in the skillet into the pot, mixing it in with the beans, and cook for 30 minutes, or until the beans are tender.

Add the zucchini, corn, tomatoes, and bouillon cubes. After 5 minutes, remove the whole tomatoes and place them in a bowl of cold water for a few minutes. Peel off the tomato skin when it's loose, then coarsely chop the tomatoes and reintroduce them to the beans.

Cook another 1 to $1^1/_2$ hours on low, adjusting the water and seasoning with salt and pepper to taste.

SERVING SUGGESTION
Serve with cornbread or biscuits, with sliced cucumbers and tomatoes on the side lightly covered with lite vinegar and oil. Summer Beans are also good over steamed rice.

New Year's Eve Black-Eyed Peas

Making peas and beans is like being a musician; it's important to get a good rhythm going and stay with it. Use the same pot for your beans every time, so you can get to know it. And cook 'em slow.

By the way, I don't give this New Year's Eve Black-Eyed Peas recipe to just anybody. It's guaranteed to bring good luck for three years. And I'm not lying this time.

MAKES 6 TO 8 SERVINGS

1 pound (2 cups) dry black-eyed peas

8 cups water

1 bay leaf

1 15-ounce can chopped tomatoes

6 bacon slices, cut in 1-inch squares

3 tablespoons flour

1 cup coarsely chopped white onions

1/2 cup coarsely chopped green or red bell peppers

1/2 cup coarsely chopped celery

2 cloves garlic, thinly sliced

salt and pepper to taste

In a large pot or your favorite bean pot, cook the peas in water over a light simmer, adjusting the water when necessary to keep the peas barely covered. If you think it's cruel and unusual punishment to cook peas alone, go ahead and add the bay leaf.

Simmer 1 to 1¹/₂ hours. Add the tomatoes to the pot.

In a skillet on medium heat, sauté the bacon. When the bacon begins to lightly brown, add the flour and sauté for 2 to 3 minutes. Add the chopped vegetables and garlic to the skillet, sautéing for 2 to 3 minutes.

Add everything in the skillet to the peas and cook 45 minutes to an hour, until the peas are really tender, adjusting the water as needed.

Remove the bay leaf and add salt and pepper to taste.

Matt's Stand-By Queso

Here's an excellent light lunch. Just pour the queso over sautéed mushrooms, roll it into some pasta, or pour it over fried rice. It's also great on hot dogs.

MAKES 4 TO 6 SERVINGS

1 tablespoon oil of your choice

3 tablespoons finely chopped white onions

2 tablespoons finely chopped red and/or green bell peppers

1 tablespoon finely chopped celery

$\frac{1}{2}$ teaspoon granulated garlic

$\frac{1}{4}$ teaspoon ground cumin

1 large jalapeño, in thick slices

$\frac{1}{2}$ cup chicken broth

1 pound shredded American cheese

Heat the oil in a large skillet over medium heat, then sauté in the onions, bell peppers, celery, garlic, cumin, and jalapeño until the onion is translucent.

Add the chicken broth and turn the heat down to low. Sprinkle in the cheese and lightly simmer until all the cheese is melted.

Big-Batch Potato Salad

It's always important to be prepared for a party because you never know when one's going to break loose. Big-Batch Potato Salad will help you satisfy your guests at potluck dinners, funerals, family reunions, and bar mitzvahs (omit the bacon, of course, for the bar mitzvahs).

MAKES 40 TO 50 SERVINGS

10 pounds red potatoes, cubed

1 dozen hard-boiled eggs, chopped

2 cups mayonnaise

¼ cup mustard

1½ cups coarsely chopped dill pickles

1 7-ounce jar pimentos

2 cups coarsely chopped celery

2 tablespoons salt

1 tablespoon black pepper

4 slices crispy bacon and drippings (optional)

paprika and parsley for garnish

In a big pot, boil the potatoes for 15 to 20 minutes, until they flake off with a fork. Drain, and chill the potatoes along with the eggs.

Combine all the ingredients in a big bowl and mix well, blending the potatoes and eggs into all else.

SERVING SUGGESTION
I usually add the bacon and drippings when nobody's watching.

Big-Happenin' Beans

Nothing like a big pot of beans for a grand occasion. These are simple and tasty.

1 pound bacon

2 cups coarsely chopped white onions

2 to 3 bay leaves

1 gallon dry pinto beans

3 gallons water

1/4 cup salt

1 tablespoon black pepper

Fry the bacon in a large stockpot until it's firm, but not crispy. Add the onions and bay leaves and cook until the onions just start to brown.

Add the beans and water and bring to a boil, then turn down the heat to a very low simmer and cook for 2$\frac{1}{2}$ to 3 hours. Continue to add water as needed to just cover the top of the beans.

Add the salt and pepper when the beans are tender. Remove the bay leaves before serving.

Fried Spicy Okra

Here's another one of those appetizers or side dishes that curses the main course. Just make this once for a fish fry, and all you're certain to hear before the next fry is, "We're going to have that okra again, aren't we?"

And we always do.

The okra gets its spiciness from the boiling.

MAKES 4 TO 6 SERVINGS

1 cup coarsely chopped white
    onions

3 cloves garlic, sliced

2 tablespoons salt

3 fresh jalapeños, quartered

3 cups water

1 pound fresh or frozen okra
    (use young pods if fresh)

3/4 cup cornmeal

1/4 cup flour

1 teaspoon black pepper

In a pot, throw in the onions, garlic, salt, and jalapeños and bring to a boil in 3 cups of water, then allow to simmer for 2 to 3 minutes.

Add the okra, and simmer until tender, about 4 or 5 minutes, being careful not to overcook the okra.

Set the okra aside to cool, while mixing the cornmeal, flour, and pepper.

Heat a skillet or deep fat fryer to approximately 375°.

Coat the okra in the flour mixture and fry it to a golden brown, approximately 2 to 3 minutes.

SERVING SUGGESTION

Fried Spicy Okra is very popular at barbecues and catfish fries.

Mom's Garden Squash

When I was growing up, Mom cooked durn near everyday in my family's Austin restaurant, El Rancho, so I spent a lot of time under the supervision of her mother, Granny Gaytan.

My granny grew many vegetables in her garden, but she took special pride in her squash. It was a summer delight.

I guess that's where my mom gets her "squash" habits. I can never make it as good as Mom or Granny Gaytan always did. Squash has just always tasted better with one of them stooped over a stove.

MAKES 4 SERVINGS

2 tablespoons butter

½ cup coarsely chopped white onions

1 clove garlic, diced

1 pound diced yellow or zucchini squash

1 cup coarsely chopped fresh tomatoes

1 diced fresh jalapeño or anaheim pepper (optional)

1 tablespoon chopped cilantro

½ teaspoon salt

2 to 3 ounces Monterey Jack or Mozzarella cheese, in strips

Melt the butter in a saucepan over low heat.

Add the onions and garlic, and sauté until the onions become soft and translucent, but not browned. This only takes 1 to 2 minutes.

Add the remaining ingredients except the cheese, and cook covered over medium heat for 10 minutes or until the squash is done, yet still firm. Drain off the water, and pour the squash into a flameproof glass dish.

Garnish with the cheese strips, and place under a broiler for 1 to 2 minutes, or until the cheese is melted.

Serve immediately.

Happy Potatoes Side Dish

You'll be happy, too, because this dish can be modified to suit your own tastes. The more you fix it, the more you learn what you want to do the next time. You might want to change the heat a little, or change the ingredients to suit your own buds. That's what cooking is all about. Spoil yourself and by all means express yourself.

MAKES 4 SERVINGS

4 8-ounce potatoes

4 tablespoons Parmesan cheese

2 strips bacon, fried and crumbled

1 tablespoon salt

$^3/_4$ tablespoon pepper

$^1/_4$ tablespoon cayenne pepper

4 tablespoons butter

4 tablespoons sour cream

Preheat the oven to 375°. Thoroughly wash and dry the potatoes, and pierce them several times with a fork. Place the potatoes on a baking sheet, and place in the oven for 1$^1/_2$ hours.

Remove the potatoes and slice them the long way in half. Make 3 to 4 slits on the flat side of each potato.

In a bowl, mix together the cheese, bacon crumbs, salt, pepper, and cayenne pepper. Sprinkle the mixture evenly over the potatoes. Spread 1 tablespoon of butter and 1 tablespoon of sour cream over each potato.

Return the potatoes to the oven for 5 more minutes.

SERVING SUGGESTION

As an alternative to the Parmesan cheese, sprinkle Cheddar, American, or Monterey Jack cheese over the potatoes. Each is a special treat. For grilling in an open fire, wrap well with foil.

Navy Beans

If you're like me, you had to acquire a taste for navy beans. I used to leave them on the plate, until my mom started giving me the look.

Somewhere along the way, navy beans and I got right with each other, and Mom's glare calmed to a flicker. These days, I cook them once a month, usually when nobody's looking.

MAKES 4 TO 6 SERVINGS

1 cup dried navy beans

4 cups water

1 ham hock or salt pork

½ cup diced white onions

2 cloves minced garlic

2 tablespoons chopped cilantro

1 cup canned tomatoes with juice

salt and pepper to taste

Thoroughly wash the beans, then place them in a heavy saucepan with the 4 cups of clear water and the ham hock or salt pork. Bring to a boil on medium to high heat, then reduce the heat to low and cover for 2 hours.

Check and stir periodically, and add water as needed to keep the beans from drying out.

After 2 hours, add the onions, garlic, cilantro, and tomatoes with juice. Cook the beans at least 10 minutes longer, or until the beans are soft and mash easily. Salt and pepper to taste.

SERVING SUGGESTION
I love a half cup of sliced, smoked German-style sausage instead of the ham hock. My favorite is New Braunfels-style sausage, if you can get your hands on some.

Sweet Peas

I have two boys who don't like sweet peas. One is gradually being converted by this method. The other one, I'm still working on.

3 tablespoons butter

1 tablespoon flour

³/₄ teaspoon salt

¹/₂ teaspoon white pepper

2 teaspoons finely chopped white onions (optional)

1 clove garlic, minced (optional)

2 cups sliced mushrooms

1 cup chicken stock or broth

2 cups frozen (or 2 cans) sweet peas

¹/₂ cup grated Parmesan cheese

1 cup half-and-half

3 to 4 teaspoons chopped parsley, as a garnish

In a large skillet, melt the butter over low heat. Blend in the flour.

Add the salt, pepper, onions, and garlic, and sauté until the onions become translucent. Add the mushrooms and sauté for 3 to 4 additional minutes, scraping the pan and mixing thoroughly.

Add the stock or broth and bring to a simmer. Add the peas, cheese, and half-and-half, and simmer on low heat for 4 to 5 minutes.

Garnish with parsley.

SERVING SUGGESTION
Leftover peas and a little white rice complement a salad and make a great lunch.

Plain Rice

It's amazing how many people can't boil regular ol' rice. Try it several times with the same pot and lid, and keep an eye on your flame.

Once you get Plain Rice down pat, all your rices will start coming out good. Keep in mind that 1 cup of raw rice equals 3 cups of cooked rice.

MAKES 4 TO 6 SERVINGS

3 cups water

1½ cups raw long grain white rice

1½ teaspoons butter or bacon drippings

STOVETOP METHOD

Bring the water to a boil over high heat, then add the rice and butter or bacon drippings.

Bring the water to a boil a second time, then place on a tight-fitting lid and cook gently for 15 minutes.

Remove the rice from the heat, and fluff it with a fork. If your stovetop is too busy at the time, try the following oven method.

OVEN METHOD

Preheat the oven to 325°. Place the water and the butter or bacon drippings in a casserole dish with a lid or an ovenproof pot with a lid.

Add the rice in 10 to 15 minutes, or when the water is heated. Place the lid tightly over the vessel, and cook the rice 25 to 30 minutes until all the water is absorbed.

Serve hot, or save for a recipe that requires rice.

SERVING SUGGESTION

This is excellent rice with gumbos (see pp. 36–41), Red Beans and Rice (see pp. 102–103), or as a side dish with any of the chicken or gravy recipes in this book.

Fancy Rice

Here's a Sunday rice, but you don't need to be wearing your church clothes to make it. The recipe calls for the chopped vegetables of your choice, but do not use any leafy veggies except cabbage. I recommend corn, peas, and onions.

1¹/₂ teaspoons butter

2 cups finely chopped vegetables of your choice

1¹/₂ cups raw long grain white rice

3 cups chicken stock (see p. 44)

salt to taste

¹/₂ teaspoon white pepper

cilantro or parsley (optional)

In your favorite 10-inch skillet, add the butter and vegetables. Add the rice, chicken stock, salt, and pepper to the skillet.

Bring to a boil, then reduce to a simmer for 15 minutes.

Remove from the heat and fluff the rice using a fork.

SERVING SUGGESTION
I love serving this with grilled or steamed vegetables such as bell peppers, carrots, or tomatoes. For added color to the rice, sprinkle in cilantro or parsley while fluffing the rice.

Old Time Dirty Rice

Dirty Rice was popularized in the backwoods, where a 10-inch skillet was almost always handy.

½ stick butter

heart, liver, and gizzard from
   1 chicken or 1 duck

2 cloves garlic, thinly sliced

1 cup thinly chopped white
   onions

¼ cup thinly sliced celery

2 cups long grain white rice

1 bay leaf

½ teaspoon salt

½ teaspoon black pepper

¼ teaspoon thyme

½ teaspoon crushed sage

4 cups chicken stock
   (see p. 44)

Place the butter in a skillet and melt over moderate heat.

Very finely chop the heart, liver, and gizzard, then add them to the skillet and sauté until the giblets are light brown.

Add the garlic, onions, and celery, and continue to sauté until the onions are translucent.

Add the rice and the seasonings, and toss for 1 minute.

Add the chicken stock and bring to a boil.

Cover and simmer for 15 minutes or until all the moisture is absorbed. Remove the bay leaf before serving.

SERVING SUGGESTION

This rice is a good side dish for the chicken or duck that donated the organs.

Creamy Sweet Corn

This side dish goes well with fish, chicken, and steaks. The kind of milk you use is really up to you.

2 tablespoons butter

2 tablespoons flour

$\frac{1}{2}$ cup finely chopped white onions

$\frac{1}{2}$ cup coarsely chopped red bell peppers

3 cups frozen or fresh corn

1 teaspoon sugar

1 cup chicken stock (see p. 44)

1 cup half-and-half or whole milk

salt and pepper to taste

paprika or parsley for garnish

Parmesan cheese (optional)

Add the butter and flour to a skillet and ever so lightly brown over moderate heat.

Add the onions and bell peppers to the skillet, and sauté for 2 minutes.

Add the corn and sugar, and sauté for 2 more minutes.

Add the chicken stock and the half-and-half or whole milk, and simmer over low heat for 5 more minutes.

Add salt and pepper to taste, and garnish with paprika or chopped parsley.

SERVING SUGGESTION

I like mine with grated Parmesan sprinkled on top just before serving.

Seasonal Grilled Vegetables

Make sure your veggies are sliced thick enough that they don't fall between your grill. They're best charred on the outside but still crunchy inside.

If you don't want to use zucchini squash or yellow squash, you may use any seasonal vegetables of your choice to equal a half-gallon in quantity.

MAKES 4 TO 6 SERVINGS

$^1/_2$ cup butter (or oil) of choice

2 cloves finely chopped garlic

$^1/_2$ cup finely chopped sweet white onions

$^1/_2$ cup coarsely chopped fresh cilantro or parsley

1 teaspoon salt

$^3/_4$ teaspoon black pepper

juice from 1 lemon or lime

1 tablespoon Kikkoman Light Soy Sauce

3 ears of corn, quartered

2 cups mushrooms of your choice

1 large zucchini squash sliced $^1/_2$-to-$^1/_4$-inch thick

2 yellow squashes sliced $^1/_2$-to-$^1/_4$-inch thick

In a large skillet, combine the butter (or oil), garlic, onions, cilantro or parsley, salt, pepper, lemon or lime juice, and soy sauce. Heat these ingredients to blend the flavors. Add the vegetables to the skillet, toss and blend.

Pour vegetables onto a medium-high to high heat grill. Put the skillet aside, and reserve it for the vegetables.

At first, watch for the vegetables to lightly flare up. Cook the vegetables on the grill for 3 to 5 minutes, turning occasionally. Return the vegetables to the skillet.

Let the vegetables sit for 3 to 4 minutes before serving.

Macaroni and Cheese

If you're making this side dish with children in mind, substitute 2 additional tablespoons of red or green bell peppers for the jalapeño.

3 tablespoons finely chopped onions

2 tablespoons finely chopped bell peppers

1 tablespoon finely chopped celery

½ teaspoon granulated garlic

¼ teaspoon cumin

1 large, thinly sliced jalapeño

½ cup chicken stock (see p. 44)

1 pound cubed or shredded American cheese

1 12-ounce package shell macaroni

2 tablespoons butter

In a saucepan, bring the onions, bell peppers, celery, garlic, cumin, and jalapeño to a boil in the chicken broth.

Turn to a simmer and add the cheese, gently cooking another 2 to 3 minutes or until the cheese is thoroughly melted. Set the cheese aside, but keep it warm.

Cook the shells according to their directions.

After the shells are done, add the butter and the still-warm cheese mix.

Toss the mixture to thoroughly coat all the shells. Serve it while it's hot.

COOKING SUGGESTION

To make a full meal, add 1 can of peas and 1 can of drained tuna to the queso mixture. You've just created tuna casserole with a bite.

CHAPTER FOUR

Main Courses

THE MAIN COURSE IS WHERE YOU WIND UP after all the fore-play. You've had your good appetizers and maybe a good cock-tail or two. You've got your sides looking good. Now it's time for the main squeeze, so to speak.

These dishes have a nice variation, including a few primi-tive touches. I realize almost any cooking style these days, whether it's Cajun, Mexican, New Mexican or Tex-Mex, shies away from organ recipes.

But I love my liver. I like a good beef tongue on occasion. Heck, I'll work up a venison or elk heart in the mornings. I'll dust it and fry it in bacon drippings and gulp it right down. That's good eating.

But, as I said, there's a little here for everybody—from Broiled Soft-Shell Crabs to The World's Largest Enchilada. Pick your favorites and have at 'em.

Broiled Soft-Shell Crabs

My wife, Estella, loves soft-shell crabs almost as much as she loves me, but we don't like them too heavily battered. Using the following formula, the crabs come out nice and crispy without bloating our bellies. They're also great appetizers.

MAKES 4 SERVINGS

1/4 cup melted butter

juice of 1 lemon

1 tablespoon lite soy sauce

1 garlic clove, crushed

8 small soft-shell crabs, cleaned and washed

1/2 cup flour

1 teaspoon salt

1/2 teaspoon white pepper

1/4 teaspoon cayenne pepper

In a skillet, heat the butter, lemon juice, soy sauce, and garlic over low heat for 2 minutes. Remove the skillet from the fire and add the crabs, tossing and coating them thoroughly in the sauce.

Place the flour, salt, pepper, and cayenne in a paper bag and shake to mix. Place the crabs in the bag and shake until each is coated on all sides.

Turn on the broiler. Place the coated crabs on a broiling rack and broil approximately 5 minutes per side, or until golden brown. Serve immediately.

SERVING SUGGESTION
Throw together some Big Dog Tartar Sauce (see p. 128) and serve on the side.

South Texas Salisbury Steak

Here's my rendition of a favorite that might date back to the Stone Ages, at least in South Texas.

MAKES 4 TO 6 SERVINGS

2 pounds round steak

1 tablespoon oil of your choice

1 teaspoon salt

$\frac{1}{2}$ teaspoon black pepper

$\frac{1}{2}$ cup flour

$\frac{1}{2}$ teaspoon granulated garlic

$\frac{1}{2}$ teaspoon cumin

1 cup coarsely chopped white onions

$\frac{1}{2}$ cup coarsely chopped celery

$\frac{1}{2}$ cup coarsely chopped green or red bell peppers

2 cups (or a 15-ounce can) fresh tomatoes

1 cup water

1 tablespoon Worcestershire sauce

Trim the fat from the steaks and cut the steaks into serving pieces. Place the oil and trimmed fat on low heat to render.

On the side, season the steaks with the salt and pepper. Sprinkle half the flour on a cutting board or counter top. Coat one side of the steaks with the flour, and add the remaining flour to the top of the steaks. Pound the steaks with a mallet or knife handle.

Remove the pieces of trimmed fat from the skillet and turn the heat up to medium. Add the steaks and brown one side for 1 to 2 minutes. Flip, and add seasonings, onions, celery, and bell peppers. Continue to brown, searing the steaks and vegetables in the skillet.

When the steaks are brown and the onions are translucent, add the tomatoes, water, and Worcestershire sauce.

Place a lid on the skillet and cook on very low heat for $1\frac{1}{2}$ hours, or until the steaks are fork tender.

Shredded Beef
(for Crock Pots and Slow Cookers)

Shredded beef can be substituted in many chicken or pork dishes, and it can also be used in many instances instead of ground meat. Working with the Texas Beef Council, I came up with over 100 ways to use shredded beef.

MAKES 8 TO 10 SERVINGS

3 to 4 pounds boneless beef roast

oil of your choice

1 medium white onion, quartered

3 to 4 cloves garlic, peeled

1 teaspoon salt

1 teaspoon pepper

$3/4$ cup water

Put everything in the slow cooker, beef first with everything else sprinkled on top. Cook on low for 9 to $9^{1}/_{2}$ hours, or until the beef is tender (or, follow your slow cooker's manufacturer's instructions for cooking time and temperatures; they vary).

Remove the beef and cool slightly. Trim and discard excess fat, then shred the beef by sticking it with two forks close together and pulling in opposite directions.

Shredded Beef
(for Roasting—Range Top or Oven)

Shredded beef is ideal for tacos, fajitas, scrambled eggs, grilled-cheese sandwiches, or for chowders instead of bacon. Here is a general rule-of-thumb for roasting.

MAKES 6 TO 8 SERVINGS

8 to 10 pound brisket, untrimmed

1 tablespoon oil of your choice

2 cups water, juice, beer, or wine

In a heavy pan, brown the beef on all sides in a small amount of the oil of your choice. Season the beef as desired. Add a small amount of water, juice, beer or wine (about 2 cups will do). Cover tightly and simmer gently over low heat on top of the range or in a 325° oven until the beef is fork-tender, about 3½ to 4 hours.

Shred the beef with two forks close together, pulling the forks away from each other.

Matt's Favorite Shredded Beef Brisket

I never season my shredded beef because it's so good about picking up the flavors of the sauces and other ingredients I use it with.

This is a very user-friendly, succulent brisket, excellent on tacos, fajitas, scrambled eggs, grilled-cheese sandwiches, or chowders instead of bacon.

MAKES 6 TO 8 SERVINGS

8 to 10 pound brisket,
untrimmed

Place the brisket in a roasting pan on a rack. Seal the roasting pan with aluminum foil and place a lid over the pan. You want to create a tight lid with a little pressure inside. Cook at 200°, 1 hour per pound, until it's almost falling apart. Shred it or slice it.

For variations, add onions and peppers and garlic around the meat, with your favorite liquid—beer or wine or water—but not enough moisture to touch the brisket. A cup or two will do.

I like to put this on at night and have it ready for me to shred for breakfast tacos in the morning. I store it in Ziploc bags, about 2 cups each.

Beef Fajitas
with Shredded Beef

Here's my Number One catering item. It's also taking my restaurants by storm. I'm the first to make fajitas with shredded beef. You can be the next in line, if you hurry.

MAKES 6 TO 8 HUNGRY SERVINGS

4 tablespoons oil of your choice

2 cups coarsely chopped white onions

1 cup coarsely chopped red or green bell peppers

4 cups cooked shredded beef (see pp. 74-76)

1 teaspoon granulated garlic

1 teaspoon salt

3/4 teaspoon pepper

2 tablespoons lite soy sauce

1 tablespoon red wine vinegar

18 flour tortillas

Heat the oil in a large skillet or griddle on high heat. Add the onions and bell peppers and sauté for 1 minute. Add the beef, garlic, salt, and pepper. Continue to sauté for 1 to 2 minutes. Taste and adjust salt and pepper.

Add soy sauce and vinegar, thoroughly mixing it in. Serve immediately inside hot tortillas heated in a skillet or over an open-flame gas burner (I don't recommend the microwave or oven for a good tortilla). When tortillas are soft, fill with beef mixture.

SERVING SUGGESTION

Best to fill tortillas with hot sauce, chili con queso, guacamole, and sour cream.

Texas Grilled-Cheese Sandwich

This is a full meal. I haven't found one child who doesn't like a grilled-cheese sandwich done the right way, including my own self.

MAKES 4 SERVINGS

2 tablespoons finely chopped green or red bell peppers

2 tablespoons finely chopped tomatoes

2 tablespoons finely chopped white onions

stick of butter

8 slices Texas toast

8 slices American cheese

1 cup cooked shredded beef (see pp. 74-76)

Combine the bell peppers, tomatoes, and onions, and set aside. Butter one side of each bread slice, and toast in a frying pan or skillet with the buttered side down.

Place one slice of cheese on the toasted side of 4 slices of bread. Place 2 tablespoons of shredded beef on each cheese slice, then spread 1½ tablespoons of the bell pepper/tomato/onion mixture over the beef.

Top with a second slice of cheese and another bread slice, with the toasted side down. Spread the butter on the untoasted side. Grill in a non-stick pan until golden brown, and the cheese is melted.

COOKING SUGGESTION

Instead of the bell peppers, tomatoes, and onions, you can substitute 6 tablespoons of pico de gallo. When the sandwiches are golden brown, I like to sprinkle on a little Parmesan cheese and flip them around in the grill a bit just before serving.

Hollandaise Grilled-Cheese Sandwich

Being a grilled-cheese freak, I'm always looking for new ways to build a grilled-cheese sandwich. This one makes me very, very happy. The secret is to cook the cheese slow and easy. It's worth the extra time.

MAKES 1 SANDWICH

2 slices of thick bread

2 tablespoons of your favorite hollandaise sauce (see Matt's Anchovy Hollandaise Sauce, p. 135)

grated Monterrey Jack, American, or your favorite cheese

In a pan, lightly toast one side of each of the bread slices. Remove the bread slices and place on a flat surface.

Spoon on one tablespoon of hollandaise sauce per slice (I do prefer my Anchovy Hollandaise Sauce). Add your favorite cheese. Close the bread slices together, pressing the cheese and hollandaise sauce inside.

Do not butter the outside slices of bread. Using a dry skillet, slowly toast each side of the sandwich.

SERVING SUGGESTION

Don't be afraid to experiment with grilled cheese. Add beef or pork and/or mushrooms. Tomatoes bring a great-tasting surprise to grilled cheese. When using tomatoes, cut the slices real thin and allow them to drain on a paper towel before adding them to the sandwich. Hot hollandaise sauce can also be used to dress toasted hamburger buns. For burgers, I love to use Matt's Hot & Spicy Hollandaise Sauce (see p. 137).

Red Pork No. 1

If this is Red Pork No. 1, you might be wondering if there's a No. 2. Well, there is. Stop by my restaurants someday and ask me. I'll tell you all about it. But this one is still No. 1 in my book.

MAKES 6 TO 8 SERVINGS

2 pounds thin pork chops

3 tablespoons oil of your choice

1/4 cup flour for dusting plus
   3 tablespoons flour

1 cup coarsely chopped white
   onions

1/2 cup coarsely chopped red or
   green bell peppers

2 garlic cloves, chopped

1 1/2 teaspoons cumin

1 1/2 tablespoons (or to taste)
   chili powder

1 teaspoon salt

1/2 teaspoon black pepper

1 15-ounce can diced tomatoes

1 8-ounce can tomato sauce

2 cups chicken broth or water

Trim the pork chops and reserve the fat in a large, heavy skillet. Add the oil and render for 10 to 15 minutes on moderate heat.

Dust the pork chops in the 1/4 cup of flour. Remove the pork fat from the skillet, and lightly brown the pork chops in the oil on moderate heat. Add the onions and bell peppers, and continue to cook on moderate heat until the onions are translucent.

Remove all but 3 tablespoons of oil from the skillet. Sprinkle 3 tablespoons of flour over the pork chops as they sauté, then add the garlic, cumin, chili powder, salt, and pepper, and sauté on moderate to light heat for 3 to 4 minutes.

Add the tomatoes, tomato sauce, and chicken broth (or water). Bring to a light simmer and cook until the pork chops are tender, approximately 45 minutes to an hour.

Adjust salt and pepper to taste.

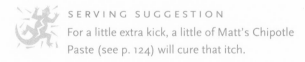

SERVING SUGGESTION
For a little extra kick, a little of Matt's Chipotle Paste (see p. 124) will cure that itch.

Matt's Answer to Dry Breasts

I haven't ordered chicken in a restaurant in a dozen years, mainly because I'm sick and tired of the boneless, breast-less, dry, stringy excuse for a chicken so often placed before me. I will pull over for some fried chicken when I'm on the road, but that's it.

Which got me to thinking. What if I used my beef technique on chicken? By golly, it comes out right every time.

This is the plumpest, juiciest way to cook boneless chicken. We'll be using the same technique in other recipes, so get it right now and this recipe will be good to you later, too.

MAKES 4 SERVINGS

4 plump chicken breasts, boneless and skinless

4 tablespoons of your favorite oil (or 1 tablespoon per breast, if cooking fewer than 4 at once)

salt and pepper to taste

flour for dusting

Thoroughly rinse and wash the chicken breasts, then lay each on a cutting board. Pound the fattest part with a meat mallet or the back of a cutting knife to 1 inch or less (do not pound the thin part).

Preheat the oven to 225°. In a large cast-iron skillet, bring the oil to moderate heat.

Salt and pepper the chicken to taste, then lightly dust each breast in flour. Put the breasts in the skillet and sauté one minute per side.

Immediately place the skillet in the oven and bake for 1 hour at 225°.

Bone-in, Skin-on Chicken

This may be the most tender, juiciest chicken you'll ever make. But you've got to practice with it, and always be sure your cooked chicken's internal temperature is at least 180°.

MAKES 4 SERVINGS

4 plump chicken breasts, bone in and skin on

4 tablespoons of your favorite oil (or 1 tablespoon per breast if cooking fewer)

salt and pepper to taste

flour for dusting

Thoroughly rinse and wash the chicken breasts while preheating the oven to 250°. Place the breasts on a cutting board, skin down, and break them on the plump end with a sharp knife or poultry shears.

Turn over each breast, place the palm of your hand on the breast and press down to further break the bone (Matt's rule of thumb: If you weigh 200 pounds, press for five seconds; if you weigh 100, press for 10 seconds). Flatten the breasts to approximately $1^1/_4$ inch.

In a large cast-iron skillet, bring the oil to moderate heat. Salt and pepper the breasts to your liking and lightly dust them in the flour. Place the breasts in the skillet and sauté for 2 minutes on each side.

Immediately place the skillet in the oven and bake the breasts for 1 hour at 250°.

Slow-Cooked Turkey Breast

Here's one for all you bakers out there. It's really, really plump.

MAKES 4 TO 6 SERVINGS

4½ to 5 pound turkey breast

1 tablespoon olive oil

1 tablespoon salt

2 teaspoons black pepper

1½ teaspoons granulated garlic

4 tablespoons flour

Set the oven to 200°. Rub breast down with olive oil.

Mix all the dry ingredients together. Sprinkle the dry mixture evenly all over the top and bottom of the breast. Place in a baking dish and cook for 6 hours.

Check the breast with a meat thermometer. When the turkey breast has an internal temperature of 180°, it should be done.

This should be the best, plumpest turkey you have ever had.

You can make this recipe using a 6-pound chicken. Cook the chicken 1 hour longer. When the internal temperature is 180°, the chicken is ready.

Cajun Turkey Breast

While I was working on my gumbos in Louisiana, this dish inspired me. I realize this is a long time to be cooking anything, so it takes a little patience. I like to put it on around noontime and have it ready for dinner. The turkey is incredibly moist and tender.

If you can maintain your barbecue pit temperature at 200° degrees, I highly recommend smoking it. But don't let the temperature slip below 200°.

MAKES 4 TO 6 SERVINGS

4½ to 5 pound turkey breast

2 tablespoons bacon drippings

rosemary or basil (a pinch)

1 tablespoon salt

1 teaspoon black pepper

1½ teaspoons granulated garlic

1 tablespoon cayenne pepper

½ teaspoon thyme

4 tablespoons flour

Set the oven to 200°. Rub breast down with bacon drippings. Sprinkle with the rosemary or basil.

Mix all the dry ingredients together. Sprinkle the dry mixture evenly all over the top and bottom of the breast. Place in a baking dish and cook for 6 hours.

Check the breast with a meat thermometer. When the turkey breast has an internal temperature of 180°, it should be done.

You can also make this recipe using a 6-pound chicken. Cook the chicken 1 hour longer. When the internal temperature is 180°, the chicken is ready.

Braised Spanish Steak

This is my spin on another Texas Beef Council classic. I like to add Chipotle Paste (see p. 124) or mix a couple of chipotle peppers in the sauce to give it a little more zing. Tabasco or Louisiana hot sauce on the side nicely complements the steak.

MAKES 4 SERVINGS

2 pounds round steak, cut into 8 pieces

2 tablespoons oil

1 15-ounce can tomatoes (with juice)

1 4-ounce can chopped green chiles

3/4 cup beer of your choice

1 tablespoon chili powder

2 teaspoons beef bouillon granules

1 cup coarsely chopped onions

2 cloves garlic, chopped

2 tablespoons flour

Brown the meat on both sides in oil in a Dutch oven. Combine the tomatoes and chiles with only 1/2 cup of the beer, as well as the chili powder, beef bouillon, onions, and garlic. Pour the mixture over the meat and bring to a boil.

Reduce the heat, cover, and simmer for 2 hours, or until tender.

Combine the remaining 1/4 cup beer and flour to make a smooth paste. Add it to the liquid in the pan to make gravy. Cook over low heat and stir until thickened.

Beef Tongue

First time I ate tongue, I was a lad. My mother had it in a skillet hanging around with some vermicelli, pinto beans, and tomato sauce. I used a flour tortilla for a scooper and some hot sauce for good measure, and it went down real good.

My taste buds got real acquainted with it, and then one day I asked some of my buddies if they'd ever eaten tongue. They made all kinds of faces but refused to bite.

So one day I mixed in some tongue while making tacos for my pals. They started going, "Mmmmmmmmmmm." Until I said, "You just ate tongue." They didn't want to admit it was as good as it was.

This is my mom's recipe. Her mother, Granny Gaytan, made it the same way, which means this is another of those dishes that has withstood the test of time.

MAKES 4 TO 6 SERVINGS

2 pounds raw beef tongue, unskinned

4 cups water (or enough to cover meat)

1 clove fresh garlic

1 teaspoon salt

Boil the tongue, covered over low heat, with the whole clove of garlic and salt for at least 2 hours, or until the meat is tender. Test for tenderness by piercing the tongue with a sharp knife or fork, as you would a roast. Remove the tongue when it's tender and let it cool.

Reserve 2 cups of broth and let it cool.

Strip the skin off the cooled tongue and trim the fat. Slice the meat into 1/4-inch medallions and set aside.

FOR THE SAUCE:

2 tablespoons vegetable oil

1/2 cup coarsely chopped white onions

1 clove fresh mashed garlic

1 heaping tablespoon flour

1 cup coarsely chopped tomatoes

1/2 cup diced bell peppers

1/2 teaspoon black pepper

1/2 teaspoon salt (optional)

1/8 teaspoon (a dash) clove

2 cups broth

SAUCE PREPARATION:

In a skillet heat 2 tablespoons of oil over medium heat.

Sauté the onions and mashed garlic for 1 minute, or until the onions are soft and translucent but not browned. Add the flour and mix into a paste. Brown a few seconds, only until the flour mixture is light brown in color, stirring constantly so that the flour paste does not scorch.

Add the tomatoes, bell peppers, black pepper, salt (if necessary), clove, and 2 cups of reserved broth, mixing thoroughly.

Bring to a hard boil, stirring constantly until the sauce starts to thicken. Add the sliced tongue and simmer for 5 more minutes.

Serve immediately with fresh flour or corn tortillas.

This goes well with sopa de arroz (Spanish rice soup).

Pollo Guisado
(Chicken and Gravy)

This is one of my mom's best recipes, and I can remember going through loaves of white bread just sopping up the gravy.

That's the good news for soppers. Despite what Miss Manners or anyone else might tell you, it's okay to sop up this particular gravy with white bread and not be chastised for poor table manners. In fact, it's bad manners leaving this gravy in the skillet. You gotta wipe it clean.

MAKES 4 SERVINGS

¼ cup vegetable oil

2 pounds fryer parts (or your favorite parts or a whole fryer)

1 teaspoon salt

1 teaspoon black pepper

1 cup diced white onions

1 large clove (or 2 medium cloves) minced fresh garlic

2 tablespoons flour

½ cup diced fresh tomatoes

1 teaspoon ground cumin

2 cups chicken broth (an additional ½ cup more, if needed)

1 cup tomato sauce

1 tablespoon coarsely chopped parsley

TO SAUTÉ THE CHICKEN:

Heat the oil in a deep, heavy skillet or Dutch oven (10-inch diameter or larger) over medium heat. While the oil heats, place the chicken pieces in a large mixing bowl and sprinkle the salt and black pepper over them. Mix the chicken pieces thoroughly, so that every piece is coated with the salt and pepper mix.

When the oil is heated, add the chicken pieces and sauté over medium heat until the pieces are browned on all sides, turning them over periodically so that all sides brown evenly. This will take 12 to 15 minutes, depending on the size of the chicken pieces.

Don't worry if the pieces stick a bit to the bottom of the skillet.

TO MAKE THE GRAVY:

Scrape the bottom of the skillet free of all sticking pieces of meat and drippings, but don't remove them because they help flavor the gravy. In the same skillet over medium heat, sauté the onions for 30 to 45 seconds.

Add the garlic and flour, mixing until a paste is formed. Sauté 1 more minute, stirring constantly until the flour turns a wheat-brown color.

Add the tomatoes, and sauté 45 more seconds while mixing thoroughly and scraping the bottom of the pan to keep the vegetables and flour paste from sticking.

Add the cumin and stir thoroughly another 30 seconds, then add the chicken broth and mix thoroughly with a wire whisk to break up any flour lumps.

When thoroughly mixed, add the tomato sauce and continue to stir with a whisk.

Bring the gravy to a boil and add the chicken pieces. Bring the chicken and gravy to a hard boil. Add the chopped parsley and turn the heat down to low. Cook over low heat 12 to 15 minutes, or until the meat falls off the bone with the slight prodding of a fork. Stir occasionally, continuing to scrape the bottom so that nothing sticks. Make sure that the chicken pieces are well soaked in the gravy.

Add a little more broth or water as necessary to thin the gravy out a bit if it thickens too much.

When done, check for any excess oil floating on the surface, and skim off as necessary.

Chicken in Green Sauce with Pumpkin Seeds

This is one of my mom's recipes, and the first time I looked over the ingredients it didn't exactly stir up my appetite—until I tasted it. Now, I consider this chicken dish the Miller Lite of all chicken dishes: It tastes great and is less filling.

MAKES 6 SERVINGS

3 pounds chicken breasts and thighs, trimmed of fat

2$\frac{1}{2}$ cups water

1 teaspoon salt

1 cup roasted pumpkin seeds

1$\frac{1}{2}$ cups fresh green tomatillos, chopped and peeled of their paper-like skin

2 cups coarsely chopped white onions

$\frac{1}{2}$ cup coarsely chopped green or red bell peppers

2 to 3 fresh serrano chile peppers

3 tablespoons fresh cilantro leaves

1 clove garlic, mashed

2 tablespoons olive oil

Place the chicken pieces, water, and salt in a large saucepan, cover, and bring to a boil.

Reduce the heat and simmer covered for 30 to 35 minutes. The meat should be almost done but not falling off the bone.

Drain the broth and reserve it, while leaving the chicken pieces in the saucepan.

Put the pumpkin seeds in a blender and blend until pulverized.

Add the tomatillos, onions, bell peppers, serranos, cilantro, garlic, and a $\frac{1}{2}$ cup of the reserved broth to the blender. Blend a few seconds at a time until you have achieved a coarse puree.

Heat 2 tablespoons of olive oil in a skillet over medium heat. Add the blender contents and sauté for a few minutes at medium heat, stirring constantly to avoid scorching.

Turn down the heat, add 1$\frac{1}{2}$ cups of the reserved broth to the skillet, and simmer on low for 10 minutes.

Pour the sauce over the chicken pieces in the pan. The sauce should be about the consistency of gravy. If the sauce is too thick, add all or part of the remaining $1/2$ cup of broth, as necessary.

Add the chicken and sauce to the skillet. Cover and cook over low heat for 20 minutes, or until the meat is tender and about to fall off the bone.

SERVING SUGGESTION

Serve with tossed salad or guacamole salad, and hot flour or corn tortillas. Or, serve with French bread or bolillos.

Chili-Roasted Sirloin with Corn Pudding

Being a beef eater, I'm in paradise working with the Texas Beef Council. Besides hanging around a bunch of great folks, I get to play with these awesome cuts of meat.

May the cow never die.

MAKES 8 TO 10 SERVINGS

FOR THE CORN PUDDING:

1 bag frozen whole kernel corn (20 oz.), defrosted

1 small onion, quartered

2 cups milk

2 eggs, beaten

8½ ounces corn muffin mix

½ teaspoon salt

1 cup Cheddar cheese, shredded

PREPARING THE CORN PUDDING:

Combine the corn and onion in a food processor bowl fitted with a steel blade. Cover and process until the corn is broken but not pureed. Scrape the side of the bowl as necessary. Add milk and eggs, and process until just blended.

Add the muffin mix and salt. Process only until mixed.

Pour the mixture into a greased 7½ x 11¾-inch baking dish. Bake in an oven at 350° for 45 to 50 minutes, or until the outside crust is golden brown.

Sprinkle with cheese and place the pudding under a broiler so that the surface is 3 to 4 inches from the heat. Broil until the cheese is melted and the top is crusty.

FOR THE SIRLOIN:

2 large cloves garlic, crushed

2 teaspoons chili powder

3/4 teaspoon dried crushed oregano leaves

1/2 teaspoon ground cumin

3 pounds boneless top sirloin steak, 2 inches in thickness

salt and pepper to taste

PREPARING THE SIRLOIN:

Combine the garlic, chili powder, oregano, and cumin, and press the mix into both sides of the steak. Place the steak on a rack in a shallow roasting pan. Do not add water or cover.

Roast the steak in a 350° oven for 50 to 60 minutes, or 16 to 20 minutes per pound. Remove when a meat thermometer inserted in the center registers 135° (for medium rare) or 150° (for medium).

Season with salt and pepper to taste.

Cover the steak with aluminum foil and let it stand 10 minutes. Carve the steak into thin slices and serve it with the Corn Pudding.

Fideo con Chorizo

How to take one giant step toward Heaven's Pearly Gates: Get yourself a good pot of pintos and some hot sauce. Then make this vermicelli, pass the corn tortillas, and praise the Lord.

3 twists of vermicelli or
  one 5-ounce box

¼ cup oil of your choice

2 links chorizo (skinned) or
  ½ pound turkey or chicken,
  cooked and cubed

½ cup coarsely chopped white
  onions

1 clove garlic, mashed

1 cup coarsely chopped
  tomatoes

½ teaspoon salt

2 cups chicken broth

One twist at a time, brown the vermicelli in hot oil in a small skillet. Fry one side, then the other, until the vermicelli is wheat-brown.

Remove the vermicelli from the skillet, lightly shaking each twist over the pan to remove the excess oil. Drain the vermicelli on paper towels.

In a small skillet, brown the chorizo (or turkey or chicken) well on low heat for 5 to 10 minutes. Stir and either crumble up the chorizo or shred the turkey or chicken.

Drain off most of the fat by squeezing the meat with the back of your spatula to remove excess grease.

Add the onions and garlic, and sauté until soft and translucent. This should take about 3 minutes over medium heat. Stir in the tomatoes and salt.

Separately bring the chicken broth to a boil, then add the meat and vegetables. Once the broth is boiling again, turn the heat to low. Break up the fideo (vermicelli) twists and drop them into the still-boiling broth. Cover and simmer 15 minutes over the low heat.

SERVING SUGGESTION
Serve in bowls garnished with your favorite grated cheese (Cheddar, Parmesan, queso fresco, and goat cheese are all good).

Matt's Mom's Huevos Rancheros

Morning romantic that I am, the smell of my Mom's Huevos Rancheros ranks right up there with fresh-brewed coffee and bacon frying in a skillet. This is as good a Mexican wakeup as you're going to find.

MAKES 2 TO 4 SERVINGS

1 tablespoon vegetable oil

¼ cup finely diced white onions

1 garlic clove, chopped
  (optional)

¼ teaspoon cumin (optional)

½ cup coarsely chopped
  tomatoes

1 or 2 coarsely chopped serrano
  chile peppers

¼ cup water

¼ teaspoon salt

2 to 4 eggs

1 tablespoon butter

First, prepare the sauce: Heat the oil in a saucepan, and sauté the onions (adding garlic and cumin if you want a bit more spice) over medium heat for 1 minute, until the onions are soft and translucent but not browned.

Add the tomatoes, peppers, and water, and cook covered over low heat for 3 minutes, stirring occasionally.

Salt to taste and set the sauce aside, keeping it warm while you cook the eggs.

Fry or scramble the eggs, as you prefer, using the butter.

Pour the sauce over the eggs and serve immediately.

SERVING SUGGESTION
Fresh flour or corn tortillas are hard to beat with huevos rancheros.

Liver No. 1

My family is not big on liver, so I usually just fix it when I'm alone and slip it into a Ziploc bag for safe keeping. That way, when I need a real good shot of organ meat, I've already got some in the freezer.

I'm not out to fool anybody. My first experience with liver was not as good as the first time I kissed Estella. But I do get a craving for both from time to time.

MAKES 4 TO 6 SERVINGS

½ pound bacon cut into 1-inch squares

2 pounds calf liver (cut into serving size pieces)

1 tablespoon salt

1 tablespoon black pepper

½ cup flour

2 cups coarsely chopped white onions

4 cloves garlic, thinly sliced

½ stick butter

2 tablespoons Kikkoman Light soy sauce

1 tablespoon sherry

1 tablespoon vinegar

In a large skillet, cook the bacon until lightly crisp, then set it aside.

Season the livers with salt and pepper, and dust with flour.

Fry the liver in the bacon drippings at a moderate heat for 2 to 3 minutes.

Add the onions, garlic, and butter, and cook for 2 to 3 minutes longer. When the onions are translucent, add the soy sauce, sherry, and vinegar.

Continue cooking for 3 to 4 more minutes.

Remove to a warm platter, and garnish with the crumpled bacon. Serve over white rice.

Chorizo con Huevos y Papas
(Mexican Sausage with Eggs & Potatoes)

This is one of my all-time favorite breakfast tacos, dating back to my youth. I can remember having these after church with a big ol' steaming cup of hot chocolate. It almost made sitting still in church worthwhile.

MAKES 4 SERVINGS

3 links chorizo or ½ pound bulk chorizo

2 tablespoons chopped white onions

1 tablespoon oil

1 tablespoon butter or margarine

1 cup boiled, diced potatoes

4 lightly beaten eggs

If the chorizo is link style, crumble and brown it in a large skillet over medium heat for 1 minute. Add the onions and mix well, letting the chorizo brown another 4 to 5 minutes. Stir regularly to avoid scorching, and make sure the chorizo is broken up well.

Remove the skillet from the heat and drain off the excess chorizo grease. Once thoroughly drained, set the chorizo aside.

In another skillet, heat the oil and butter (or margarine) over medium heat, taking care not to brown it. Once it starts sizzling, add the potatoes and cook over medium heat for 3 to 4 minutes, until the potatoes start to brown. Stir as necessary to avoid scorching, but not constantly.

Add the chorizo and onions, and cook 1 to 2 more minutes until the chorizo is thoroughly reheated.

Add the beaten eggs over medium heat until the eggs set. Then turn the eggs over, turn off the heat, and let the eggs set a few more minutes.

SERVING SUGGESTION

Serve immediately on a warm platter, with hot fresh flour or corn tortillas and fresh hot sauce. Refried beans are usually served with this dish.

Midnight Oyster Miga Omelet

Sometimes I come home late, filled with the spirit of Jack Daniel's and overcome by a few little ol' hunger pangs. These omelets help me go into the deep slumber my body needs. I figure it'll have similar results on you.

It also softens the blow in the morning, when the spirits are trying to flee your head as your eyes first squint open. Finish your day with this treasure from the sea.

MAKES 3 TO 4 SERVINGS

4 slices bacon cut into 1-inch squares

4 corn tortillas

1 cup finely chopped onions

2 cloves garlic, thinly sliced

1 thinly sliced jalapeño

1 pint drained oysters

$^1/_2$ cup chopped fresh tomatoes

$^3/_4$ teaspoons salt

$^1/_2$ teaspoon pepper

4 eggs

$1^1/_2$ cups shredded Monterey Jack cheese

Preheat the oven to 400°.

In a cast-iron (or otherwise oven-proof) skillet, fry the bacon until it is crisp, then drain the bacon on paper towels. Leave approximately 3 teaspoons of drippings in the skillet.

Cut or tear the tortillas into one-inch pieces, and fry them in the skillet with the bacon drippings until the tortillas are gently crisp. Add the onions, garlic, and jalapeños. Sauté until the onions are translucent.

Chop the oysters in halves or quarters, and sprinkle them evenly throughout the pan without mixing them into the other ingredients.

Mix together the tomatoes, salt, pepper, and eggs. Add the tomato/egg mixture to the skillet, pouring the mixture evenly across the pan without mixing. Add the cheese, and place the skillet in the oven 3 to 4 minutes, allowing the eggs to set.

SERVING SUGGESTION

Serve with sliced tomatoes with vinegar and oil. Sprinkle with cilantro.

Romantic Migas

When Estella and I are at home alone, I like to feed her these migas. They make her happy, so consequently I'm happy.

MAKES 2 SERVINGS

¹/₄ cup oil of your choice

4 soft, thin corn tortillas, cut into eighths

1 teaspoon butter

2 tablespoons coarsely chopped onions

1 tablespoon coarsely chopped bell peppers

2 tablespoons coarsely chopped tomatoes

4 eggs, beaten with a pinch of salt

Heat the oil in the skillet to medium and fry the tortilla strips until they are wheat-brown. Drain and dab the strips on paper towels. Leave 1 teaspoon of oil in the skillet.

Add the butter, onions, bell peppers, and tomatoes. Sauté over medium heat for 30 seconds.

Add the beaten eggs to the vegetables and mix briefly. Add the tortilla chips and mix again. When the eggs set, the migas are ready. Salt to taste.

SERVING SUGGESTION
Serve on a warm platter accompanied by refried beans, sausage, or bacon.

Rabbit with Chile Ancho Sauce

Over the years, I've realized there are a great many more chicken hunters than rabbit hunters. So don't forget this recipe works with chicken, as well.

Special secret: Mix in 1 teaspoon of smooth peanut butter just before serving. Your guests will swear you're a genius, and you just might be.

MAKES 4 SERVINGS

2 tablespoons oil of your choice

2 pounds rabbit or chicken cut into serving pieces

2 tablespoons flour

1 cup finely chopped onions

2 cloves garlic, mashed

1 cup chopped fresh tomatoes

½ cup coarsely chopped red or green bell peppers

2 to 3 tablespoons chili powder to taste

2 ancho chiles, made into paste

1⅓ cups chicken or beef stock

½ teaspoon ground cumin

1 teaspoon salt

Heat the oil in a large skillet over medium heat until hot, then brown the rabbit (or chicken) pieces evenly on all sides, turning the pieces to avoid scorching. When the meat has browned, which should take about 10 minutes, set it aside.

Add the flour to the remaining oil in the skillet, and brown to a paste over medium heat approximately 1 minute. Stir constantly to avoid scorching.

Add the onions and garlic to the skillet, and sauté another 2 to 3 minutes.

Add the tomatoes, bell peppers, chili powder, ancho chile paste, chicken stock, cumin, and salt, mixing all ingredients together.

Add the meat, making sure all pieces are thoroughly covered in sauce.

Turn the heat down to low and cover the skillet. Cook for 45 minutes to an hour, or until the meat is tender and about to fall off the bone.

Some rabbits are tougher than others and therefore require a longer cooking time. Always test the meat for tenderness before serving.

SERVING SUGGESTION
Serve this dish with a green salad and the fresh-cooked beans of your choice.

Red Beans and Rice No. 1

Cajuns are world famous for their comfort food. Here's a dish that's tough to beat.

1 pound salt pork or bacon

2 cups coarsely chopped white onions

2 cups (1 pound) red beans

2 quarts water

salt and pepper to taste

In a large pot, sauté the salt pork or bacon over low to medium heat for 3 to 4 minutes, until almost cooked. Add the onions and sauté until the onions are translucent.

Add the beans and water, and cook for 2½ to 3 hours over low heat using a loose fitting pot lid. For thicker beans, use a bean masher or a spoon back to stroke a couple of times and break the beans up.

SERVING SUGGESTION
Serve red beans over steamed or fried rice.

Red Beans and Rice No. 2

There are several variations of this recipe. I, for one, like red beans over a slice of fresh, fluffy corn-bread. Or, try this recipe using pinto beans instead of kidney beans. If you prefer navy beans, add one 15-ounce can of tomato sauce during the last 30 minutes of the cooking process.

For spicier beans, crush the jalapeños one at a time into the beans, sampling as you go to determine how intense you want the fire in your mouth. Simply continue to add jalapeño until you reach the desired heat.

MAKES 6 TO 8 SERVINGS

2 cups (1 pound) red kidney beans

1 pound salt pork, cut into 1-inch cubes

2 cups coarsely chopped onions

1 cup coarsely chopped green or red bell peppers

1/2 cup coarsely chopped celery

1 bay leaf

1/4 teaspoon thyme leaves

3 cloves garlic sliced

2 quarts water

4 fresh whole jalapeños (optional)

salt and pepper to taste

Wash and pick through the beans.

In a big pot, sauté the pork on low to moderate heat for 3 to 4 minutes, until it's almost cooked. Add the vegetables and spices, and sauté until the onions are translucent.

Add the water (and jalapeños, if desired) and bring it to a boil, then lower to a simmer. Gently cook the beans 2½ to 3 hours using a loose fitting pot lid.

Once the beans are tender, remove the bay leaf, and salt and pepper to taste.

SERVING SUGGESTION
Serve over steamed or fried rice.

Shrimp Miga Omelet

When the shrimp meets the tortilla, there's every reason for a happy brunch or breakfast. Or, an excellent midnight snack.

MAKES 3 TO 4 SERVINGS

4 corn tortillas, cut into 1-inch pieces

1 teaspoon vegetable or olive oil

2 tablespoons butter

1 cup coarsely chopped white onions

2 cloves garlic, thinly sliced

1 4-ounce can New Mexican green chiles or ¼ cup green or red bell peppers

1 pound raw, shelled shrimp (chopped into ¼-inch cubes, if jumbo)

1½ cups shredded Monterey Jack cheese

¾ teaspoon salt

½ teaspoon pepper

4 eggs

Preheat the oven to 400°.

In a cast-iron skillet or other oven-proof skillet, sauté the tortilla pieces in the oil until they are crisp or brown.

Add the butter, onions, garlic, and chiles or peppers, and cook until the onions are translucent.

Add the shrimp and sauté for 2 minutes.

Add the cheese, salt, and pepper to the eggs and scramble them. Add the cheese/egg mixture to the skillet. Pour the mixture evenly across the pan, but do not mix.

Place in the oven for 3 to 4 minutes, allowing the eggs to set and the cheese to melt.

SERVING SUGGESTION

Serve with your favorite salsa on the side, and even a favorite fruit.

Simple, Easy Chicken Mole

This dish is probably responsible for some of the stretch marks on my belly. It was a Sunday special once or twice a month in my childhood. We had it with Spanish rice, flour tortillas, beans, and rice. This is my dear ol' Mom's own recipe.

MAKES 4 SERVINGS

4 cups water

2 pounds chicken breast halves

¼ cup coarsely chopped white onions

¼ cup coarsely chopped celery

¼ cup chopped green bell peppers

1 teaspoon salt

2 tablespoons oil of your choice

2 tablespoons flour

2 tablespoons chili powder

2 tablespoons creamy peanut butter

1 tablespoon roasted sesame seeds

1 teaspoon granulated garlic

1 teaspoon paprika

1 teaspoon ground cumin

½ teaspoon sugar

In a large saucepan, place the 4 cups of water, chicken breasts, onions, celery, bell peppers, and a pinch of salt.

Bring to a boil, then reduce heat to low. Cover and simmer 20 to 30 minutes, or until the chicken is tender.

Remove the chicken from the broth and let it cool. Reserve the broth and vegetables.

Skin, bone, and shred the chicken.

In a large skillet, heat the oil over medium heat. Mix the flour into the oil to form a paste. In a few minutes, it will turn light brown. Stir constantly to avoid scorching.

Add the chili powder, peanut butter, sesame seeds, garlic, paprika, cumin, salt, and sugar. Mix in the broth and simmer for 5 minutes.

Add the cooked chicken, and simmer 5 more minutes.

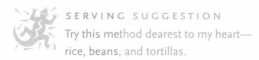
SERVING SUGGESTION
Try this method dearest to my heart—
rice, beans, and tortillas.

Mom's Turkey Meatballs

Fix these once, Mom's way, and you'll never make another Swedish meatball. They're also great appetizers for 6 to 8.

FOR THE MEATBALLS:

2 pounds ground turkey

2 tablespoons finely chopped white onions

$\frac{1}{2}$ teaspoon granulated garlic

$\frac{1}{2}$ teaspoon ground cumin

2 eggs

1 teaspoon salt

1 slice white bread, soaked in milk

1 tablespoon masa harina (flour)

FOR THE SAUCE:

3 peppers plus 2 tablespoons sauce from a 7-ounce can of chipotle peppers

$\frac{1}{2}$ cup water

$2\frac{1}{2}$ cups chicken broth

2 cups finely chopped tomatoes

$\frac{1}{4}$ cup finely chopped carrots

$\frac{1}{4}$ cup finely chopped celery

$\frac{1}{3}$ cup finely chopped cilantro leaves

$\frac{1}{2}$ teaspoon salt

Mix all meatball ingredients thoroughly and form into meatballs about the size of golf balls. This recipe should yield 18 meatballs.

For the sauce, blend the chipotle peppers and their sauce with the water. Cover and simmer over medium heat for 5 minutes.

Add the meatballs and remaining sauce ingredients, and simmer covered over low heat for 25 to 30 minutes, until the vegetables are soft. Stir every few minutes to avoid scorching.

COOKING SUGGESTION

If you like spicy food, use the entire 7-ounce can of chipotle peppers and sauce. For milder meatballs, use just 2 peppers and 1 teaspoon of the sauce. Serving hint: Leftovers can be frozen in Ziploc bags and are delicious reheated.

Matt's Turkey Balls

These are not like mountain oysters or turkey fries, so relax.

½ cup bread crumbs (1 biscuit or cornbread works great)

1 pound ground turkey

3 tablespoons minced onions

2 tablespoons bell peppers

2 tablespoons celery

1 clove garlic

¾ teaspoon salt

½ teaspoon black pepper

Preheat the oven to 400°.

Combine all the ingredients and make 18 to 20 meatballs.

Place in an ungreased 15 x 10-inch jellyroll pan or cookie sheet.

Bake 13 to 15 minutes.

Cut in half and test to make sure color is consistent.

Wino Quail

I heard this story long ago around a campfire on a quail hunting trip, but I can't tell you where or when. It's just never left me.

This ol' hunter had a dog named Hopalong, who took ill after hunting season. The veterinarian apologized and said he was going to have to put Hopalong down.

"In that case," the hunter said, "let me have him just a few more days, so we can say our goodbyes."

He took the dog hunting one more time so he could shoot just one more quail with his dog. Sure enough, he spotted one and pointed. The hunter flushed and shot the quail.

Back they went to the vet. The man laid his hunting jacket under Hopalong's head and placed that last shotgun shell near the dog's nose. Then he laid the quail nearby.

The vet did his duty, and the hunter watched his dog drift away with those familiar smells around him.

The hunter buried Hopalong near a big flat rock where they used to hunt, and placed the shotgun shell and quail in the ground with the dog.

Then came the next season and a new pup. The hunter took the pup over to where Hopalong was buried and let him sniff around awhile.

"You got some big shoes to fill," the hunter said. "But now, at least I know the spirit of the old dog will be with us all season."

MAKES 4 TO 6 SERVINGS

1/2 stick butter

6 whole quail or 8 breasts

3 tablespoons flour

3/4 teaspoon salt

1/2 teaspoon white pepper

2 cups coarsely chopped onions

2 cups coarsely chopped
  mushrooms

3 garlic cloves, thinly sliced

1 bay leaf

1/8 teaspoon thyme leaves

1 cup chicken stock

1 cup dry white wine

1 cup half-and-half or heavy
  cream

chives or parsley (for garnish)

In a Dutch oven or other large pot, melt the butter over moderate heat. Dust the quail in flour and seasonings and place them in the pot.

Add the onions, mushrooms, garlic, bay leaf, and thyme leaves.

Toss and scrape the birds along with the other ingredients in the pot for 3 to 4 minutes, cooking until the onions are translucent.

Add the stock and the wine.

Cook ever so gently with the lid on for 1 to 1 1/2 hours, watching the broth so it does not get dry.

Add water as needed and continually scrape the bottom of the pot. If the sauce is too thick, you may also add the water until you reach the desired consistency.

When the birds are tender add the cream and gently simmer 3 to 4 more minutes. Remove the bay leaf and salt and pepper to taste. Garnish with chopped chives or parsley. Serve over rice.

Mustard Catfish

Sometimes I get such a hankering for catfish I'll go to any means to eat one.

I can offer no better proof than in the late 1970s when my old bud Robert Summano and I headed out for Onion Creek south of Austin.

I knew some good fishing holes where the waters were swollen, so Robert and I placed a flat-bottom boat, some worms, crawfish, and four fishing poles in the back of my pickup and headed out.

As we paddled downstream about a mile, we noticed the water was rising slightly. We tied the boat to an old log and started fishing.

Pretty soon, the water started changing colors, getting muddier and murkier. Before we knew it, the creek had risen and was flowing swiftly.

I cut the line to the log, and we decided to float to where Highway 35 crossed over Onion Creek.

About halfway there, the boat capsized in the current. Robert and I hung onto each side of the boat as the water whisked us down the creek.

A big cypress tree smack in the water said whoa. The boat wrapped around the tree like a horseshoe, and we lost everything. The current even jerked our shoes off as we clung to each end of the boat.

Yes, it was a little brisk.

With the water still rising, there was nothing left for us to do except try to swim to the bank about 25 or 30 yards away. We crawled out on a long branch and jumped in and started swimming.

Robert and I were swept down creek another 100 yards before we made it to the bank. We had to walk four miles barefoot back to the truck, over stickers and sharp rocks.

We avoided a few snakes along the way and were badly in need of beer and food when we reached the truck. Our first stop was the first store we saw. It was then that we realized we had no wallets and no money.

As desperate as we looked, the store clerk said, "Take the six-pack. We'll get even another time."

Lone Star never tasted any better.

Nor did store-bought catfish.

I grew up eating my fried catfish with good ol' yellow mustard. To me, it gives the fish more flavor than cocktail sauce or ketchup or tartar sauce, though Mom's Tartar Sauce (p. 127) ain't too shabby.

I got stuck on this recipe a long time ago. You won't believe how good it is. You'll never even know the mustard is on the fish, but the flavor is tremendous.

MAKES 6 TO 8 SERVINGS

1 cup yellow mustard (I prefer French's)

¹/₄ teaspoon cayenne pepper

¹/₂ teaspoon black pepper

1 teaspoon salt

¹/₄ teaspoon granulated garlic

3 pounds catfish fillets, cut in ¹/₂-inch strips

2 to 2¹/₂ cups yellow cornmeal

oil of choice for frying (I recommend hog lard; peanut oil works great; do *not* use olive oil)

Mix all of the ingredients except the catfish, cornmeal, and oil. Thoroughly coat the catfish strips in the mixture, then roll in the cornmeal.

In a large skillet (black cast-iron is best), heat the oil to 375° or until it "pops" when a drop of water is added.

Add a few pieces of fish at a time, frying each for 3 to 4 minutes.

Drain the catfish on paper towels.

SERVING SUGGESTION
Eat 'em while they're hot, with ketchup or Mom's Tartar Sauce (see p. 127).

Po' Boy's Filet Mignon

If you think bacon is good on a hamburger, wait'll you wrap one around a hot dog.

Every chance I get, I like to mix in a recipe that might even strike the fancy of a young boy or girl. Cooking is easy, if you let it be. And recipes aren't always these fancy things for Fancy Dans.

Regardless of your age, try this Po' Boy's Filet Mignon. You'll feel like you're walking on sunshine.

MAKES 1 HOT DOG

1 slice bacon per dog

jumbo hot dogs of your choice

pickled jalapeños to taste

flour tortillas

toothpicks

condiments of choice (onions, relish, mustard, or ketchup)

Pound out the bacon slices until they are thin. Slice the hot dogs three-fourths down the middle, lengthwise. Spoon some pickled jalapeños along the slit.

Tightly wind the uncooked bacon strip around the hot dog, being careful not to tear the bacon. Secure the bacon with toothpicks.

Place the hot dog on low heat on a grill or in a skillet. Be patient, because the secret is in the slow cooking. The dogs may split, and some jalapeños may fall out. Not to worry—the Po' Boy's Filet Mignon is already flavored.

When the bacon is crispy, it's show time!

Grill the flour tortillas on a grill or in a skillet. Never, ever microwave your tortillas.

Remove the toothpicks from the dog. Wrap your dog in a flour tortilla, and garnish your favorite way.

Fried Oysters

My biggest problem with oysters is that I usually eat them all before I get them breaded and fried. If you can hang on long enough to fry a few, you will not be disappointed.

MAKES 4 SERVINGS

oil of your choice for deep frying
(hog lard is best; corn oil
works great, too)

1 cup yellow cornmeal

1/2 teaspoon salt

1/2 teaspoon black pepper

1/4 teaspoon cayenne pepper

1 tablespoon cornstarch

1 pint fresh drained oysters

Heat the oil to 380°.

Combine all the dry ingredients, then roll the oysters in the mixture. Drop into the hot oil.

Fry each oyster for 2 to 3 minutes, or until golden brown. Be careful not to overcook.

Drain the oysters on paper towels, and serve with ketchup, Mom's Tartar Sauce (see p. 127), or your favorite cocktail sauce.

Big Mack Chicken and Rice
(Where the Rubber Meets the Road)

You Big Arch lawyers out there calm down. This has nothing to do with your burgers. My story instead concerns an occasion when the chicken ended up where the rubber meets the road.

My mother-in-law, Nicanora Benavidez, inspired this recipe back in the early days of my romancing Estella, on one of our visits to her parents' little wood-frame house in the open country outside of Corpus Christi, Texas.

I was relaxing in the living room rocking chair, chatting with Estella's mom, who was maybe halfway through knitting a quilt while sitting on the couch.

It was a pleasant afternoon. I could see Estella's dad through the back door, plowing the field as a nice sea breeze wafted past, giving the inside of the house a crisp feel.

Out front, we heard a loud squawk, and a thump.

I sat there and watched this little ol' frail woman hop up and drop her knitting on the couch. She leaped over the coffee table and dashed into the front yard.

A Big Mack semi truck had run over one of their Rhode Island hens. The driver kept going; they don't normally stop and render aid to chickens.

The way Nicanora ran out into the road, I thought it must have been one of their prize hens. But upon returning, she calmly carried it through the house, into the kitchen, and plucked those feathers faster and prettier than I've ever seen.

When she got the water boiling and dunked that ol' chicken into the pot, I figured she was just washing off the tracks from the semi. Instead, she gave it a good cleaning, then cut the chicken into little pieces and went about preparing it to cook.

Obviously in the company of a pro, I bowed my head that evening at the supper table and filled my belly with the best durned ol' chicken and rice I've ever eaten.

To my best recollection, Big Mack Chicken and Rice goes something like this.

MAKES 6 SERVINGS

3 tablespoons vegetable oil

1½ cups uncooked long grain white rice

1 pound boned and skinless chicken meat, ground chicken or ground turkey

¾ cup finely chopped onions

½ cup celery

½ cup chopped bell pepper

1½ teaspoons salt

2 teaspoons ground cumin

1½ teaspoons granulated garlic

½ teaspoon black pepper

1 8-ounce can tomato sauce

3 cups water or chicken broth

Heat the oil in a skillet and sauté the rice until it is golden brown.

Add the chicken, vegetables, and all the spices. Continue to sauté until the chicken is slightly seared and the onions are translucent. This takes 3 to 4 minutes.

Add the tomato sauce and either the water or the broth, and bring to a boil.

Cover the skillet and simmer for 15 minutes or until the water is absorbed. The chicken should be very tender.

Remove from the heat and let the dish sit for 2 to 3 minutes.

Fluff the rice and serve.

The World's Largest Enchilada

In 1986 while living in Vail, Colorado, I orchestrated the building of the world's largest enchilada.

The Vail locals were not all that fond of Texas tourists, but they always cried when Texans didn't show up to spend their money. Their biggest beef is that we exaggerate everything.

Texas was celebrating its 150th anniversary that year, and I was trying to figure out some way to honor the occasion while operating a restaurant, Matt's Café and Cantina, inside a hotel.

I kept my prices the same in the winter months as in the summer, so the locals liked me and used the cantina as a hangout. Over a few cocktails one evening, I informed them I intended to build the world's largest enchilada in honor of the great state of Texas.

They asked how big, and I said, "Aw, just a little ol' 15-footer, probably."

A snoopy reporter came by a few days later and said, "Word's going around town that you're going to make a 150-foot enchilada."

Those Coloradans could apparently exaggerate pretty good themselves, but I tried not to blink too hard.

"I don't know where you heard that," I said.

"You backing down?" the reporter asked.

Well, that got my ire up.

"I'm not backing down, I'm stepping up. I meant to say 150 yards. I wouldn't waste my time with a wormy ol' 150-footer. I'm talking yards. One yard for every year Texas has been a state."

Obviously, this is not the sort of thing you set out to do by yourself. There were these friendly Swedes who worked in my restaurant during the winter so that they could ski all season before returning home. About a dozen of them volunteered.

Next, I set up a deal with the Blind Skiers' Association to have every foot of that enchilada auctioned off to charity.

I called the Vail Health Department and asked if they had any problems, but nobody could recollect anyone building a 150-yard enchilada before. They figured it would be okay to lay some tin foil on benches and go from there.

I got the city to plow the snow off an area of a local golf course, and the Swedes and I set up the tables and went about rolling out roughly 200 yards of tin foil.

The media, of course, was all over the story. On the eve of the event, I was asked how long it would take a good team to complete our task.

"Three to four hours," I said. "We're starting at eight tomorrow morning. Ya'll just come on by around noon. Lunch should be ready."

Three Swedes laid down the tortillas, three more put the cheese inside, three poured chili on top, and three were used to run whiskey to make sure our assembly line didn't freeze up or suffer any anxiety attacks.

We built that enchilada in 58 minutes. Somehow, through the bends and curves, it picked up eight yards along the way; but, we weren't about to make a big deal over a few extra yards.

People were coming at us from all directions. I sold the first foot and last foot of that enchilada for $500 apiece and every foot in-between for $5. Every bit of it was bought right up, and those Swedes and I were rolling around in the snow, still passing the whiskey, when most of the media arrived.

"Thought you said it was going to take three to four hours," they said.

"No, I said it would take a good crew three to four. This is a great crew."

The fine people of Vail have asked me to return and build another one, but I'm going to wait for Texas' 200th birthday so I can build a 200-yard enchilada.

You might want to work on this little 150-yarder in the meantime, but do not try this in your own front yard. It'll make the neighbors restless.

SERVES 1 SMALL VILLAGE

---

60 banquet tables

600 feet of foil (approximately)

6 to 8 large rolls masking tape

750 7-inch tortillas

190 pounds grated cheese

90 gallons chili (approximately)

Lay the tables end to end.

Lay out the foil over the tables and hold down with the masking tape.

Line up the tortillas on the table with a two-inch over-lap of one tortilla over the other, taking care to lay the last tortilla on the previous one so they are overlapped.

(continued)

Place two ounces of cheese in the first tortilla. Eyeball it, and try to put the same amount in each tortilla.

Starting from the end where you finished filling the tortillas with cheese, begin rolling each tortilla where it hooks up to the next tortilla.

Get the chili hot and pour it into as many pitchers as you can find. Pour just enough chili over the tortillas to cover them.

Go back over the tortillas with the rest of the cheese, again putting two ounces of cheese over each tortilla.

The enchilada must be made at 20°F or -4°C (obviously this is a winter sport).

Build a little fire. Drink a little whiskey.

Wait for the enchilada to freeze. When the enchilada is firm, wrap it in foil.

Sell by the foot for your favorite charity.

COOKING SUGGESTION

When ready to cook a portion of the enchilada, cook at 350° for 15 to 20 minutes until the enchilada is hot and bubbly. If you do a good enough job on this little one, I might consider you for my assembly line come Texas' 200th anniversary.

CHAPTER FIVE

Toppings and Sauces

As you enjoy your time in my favorite room—the kitchen—remember that the incredible accents to most dishes in this book are born out of the toppings and sauces you choose. And I do mean for you to do the choosing.

Look at it this way: A cowboy does not have to wear the same hat and boots everyday; or a socialite, the same jewelry. Therefore, do not simply follow my lead; lead yourself. On occasion, swap out a different sauce for the one recommended.

I mean, what's more fun, a cookbook you have to follow ingredient for ingredient, word for word; or, one that also allows you to be the mother of your own inventions? These sauces will jog your creative juices; and, as you perfect the toppings, your guests will regard you with envy and perhaps include you in their wills.

Sometimes just mixing a certain sauce into regular ol' sour cream or mayonnaise will spin you into a whole 'nuther world of tastes and flavors. It'll make dead soup walk again. The key is to use your imagination—but moderately at first, until you understand the power of what you're using. You'll be kicking up your heels in no time.

Matt's Jalapeño Paste

As all my pals have found out the hard way, I get so excited about hunting that I can't sleep the night before. Usually, no one seems to mind staying up with me, spinning yarns and pouring down social cocktails that often come in cold bottles or cans.

But 'long about 1979, five buddies turned on me during a deer hunt at a lease near the South Texas town of Freer.

I had worked late that night and did not arrive until 2 A.M., only to discover that I'd been locked out of the cabin. I knocked and knocked, but nobody would let me in because they knew I'd keep them up.

One of them finally yelled at me to sleep in the truck, and I planned on doing just that. But the night turned nippy, and while I shivered in the truck I was none too pleased to notice a beautiful stream of smoke dancing out of the cabin roof's stovepipe.

I got back up and searched through the provisions I had brought for a week's worth of cooking and came across a gallon jar of jalapeños that was just begging to be used. I climbed up on the roof and nestled up close to the stovepipe with that jar of jalapeños. I'm telling you, the smell of mesquite smoke was grand.

They must have been nice and cozy inside, when I dumped the jar's entire insides down the stovepipe. As soon as those jalapeños and the acid from the vinegar hit those toasty coals, the house came to life.

The front and back doors blew open at the same time. I even witnessed a couple of beautiful swan dives off the front porch.

I hopped off the roof and grabbed my sleeping bag and figured to get some indoor shut-eye once the fumes subsided. But the rest of the troops tackled me, rolled and stuffed me inside the sleeping bag, and nailed the bag to the cabin floor so that I could not get out.

The worst part of the entire ordeal is they went hunting the next morning and just left me there. I was madder than a wet hen with mites, and it took me forever to work myself free. When I did, I figured to heck with them and drove off toward my home in Austin.

On the way back through Freer, I noticed a hardware store was having a going-out-of-business sale. Among the items going cheap were 15 trigger-guard locks for rifles and pistols. I bought all they had and returned to camp.

My pals had their laughs and I remained chipper for a day, but that night I snuck out of bed at 2 A.M. and applied a trigger-guard lock to every gun and pistol they had brought to camp.

I was first to rise the next morning and was out in the woods when I heard all kinds of yelling and screaming and cursing and carrying on. I returned and informed them that I had all the keys to those locks, and we were going to sign a truce then and there that all was forgotten. No more retaliation.

As soon as everybody signed the paper, I told them which well I had dropped the keys in.

Turns out, it took a Freer gunsmith four hours to undo all those locks. By then, I was in my warm, cozy home in Austin, Texas, remembering that he who laughs last laughs loudest.

Speaking of jalapeños, I love this paste so much I'm going to show you how to make a bunch of it. Most cookbooks don't offer big-batch servings, but I've always been contrary to ordinary. Some sauces keep great in your refrigerator and prevent you from having to make small portions several times.

This basting sauce, or side dish, requires a smoker but is well worth the extra effort. I like to use it for rubbing down chicken, fish, steak, and pork before I put them in a smoker.

And it's not too shabby on the side, used like you would a cranberry sauce or mint jelly. It'll also give your Bloody Marys a pleasant kick.

Just don't go pouring it down any stovepipes.

MAKES 18 TO 20 SERVINGS

2 cups coarsely chopped jalapeños

1 cup coarsely chopped white onions

¼ cup fresh chopped garlic

⅔ cup oil of your choice

⅓ cup white cider vinegar

1 tablespoon salt

1 bay leaf

Get your smoker going with pecan or hickory wood until the fire is completely happy, then place all the ingredients in a pie plate and smoke for 2 to 3 hours. Leave the plate uncovered (the lid on the smoker will hold in the flavors).

After removing the plate from the smoker, discard the bay leaf and blend.

Serve hot or cold. The paste will keep in the refrigerator for several weeks if covered and sealed.

SERVING SUGGESTION

For hot dogs and hamburgers, add 1 teaspoon of Jalapeño Paste to 1 cup of mustard, mayonnaise, ketchup, or barbecue sauce. Blended with mustard, it's perfect on fried fish. Use it instead of tartar sauce.

Matt's Chipotle Paste

This Chipotle Paste has the same goal in life as the preceding Jalapeño Paste, which is to give your food a distinct personality without being overbearing, and it doesn't require a smoker. Once you start using it on chicken and ribs, you may never use anything else. I use this paste to give my barbecues and tomato sauces their special spunk.

The chipotle introduces a new way to cook. It's super on everything, from juicy steaks to juicy hot dogs and burgers.

As with the Jalapeño Paste, it's best to go easy and use only enough Chipotle Paste to keep yourself satisfied. You don't want to change the character of what you're putting it on. A little bit goes a long way.

MAKES 20 TO 30 SERVINGS, DEPENDING ON USE

6 ounces dry chipotle peppers

3 cups water

1/4 cup fresh garlic

2/3 cup oil of your choice

1/3 cup white cider vinegar

2 cups ketchup

Snip off the ends of the chipotle peppers as closely to the stems as possible. Make a slit lengthwise down the middle of each pepper and remove all the seeds.

Add the chipotle peppers and water to a saucepot and simmer on low heat for 15 to 20 minutes.

Add all the other ingredients and simmer for another 15 to 20 minutes on low heat.

Allow the mix to cool, then place it in a blender and blend it into a paste. Continue to add just enough water that the chipotle will blend all the way to the top.

My Chipotle Paste keeps indefinitely in the freezer, but I say use it when it's fresh—right after you make it.

SERVING SUGGESTION

Matt's Chipotle Paste is a great enhancer to store-bought barbecue sauce. You'll see some eyes light up; a little dab will do them.

Parsley Sauce

Here's a sauce good over vegetables, fish, chicken, and eggs.

2 tablespoons flour

2 tablespoons butter

1 cup whole milk

$\frac{1}{2}$ teaspoon white pepper

1 tablespoon sour cream

2 tablespoons finely chopped fresh parsley

1 finely chopped hard-boiled egg

Bring some water to a simmer in a double boiler. In the top pan, whisk the flour and butter, and let it sit for 2 minutes.

Stir in the milk and whisk until it's thick and smooth. Add the remaining ingredients and stir for 2 to 3 minutes. Serve on the side in a warmed sauce bowl.

COOKING SUGGESTION
If the sauce is too thick for your taste, add 1 tablespoon of water, sherry, or white wine.

Dill and Caper Sauce

One of my all-time favorites, this is a variation on a basic white sauce that hits the spot on chicken, fish, eggs, and vegetable dishes.

MAKES 4 TO 6 SERVINGS

2 tablespoons flour

2 tablespoons butter

1 cup whole milk

½ teaspoon salt

¼ teaspoon white pepper

1 tablespoon sour cream

1 tablespoon fresh dill

1 tablespoon chopped capers

1 finely chopped hard-boiled egg

Get the water simmering at the bottom of a double-boiler, then whisk the flour and butter in the top pan for 2 to 3 minutes.

Allow the flour/butter mix to sit for 2 minutes, then stir in the milk until it's smooth and thick. Add the remaining ingredients and stir for 2 to 3 minutes. Serve in a warmed sauce bowl.

COOKING SUGGESTION

Dill and Caper Sauce responds beautifully to 1 tablespoon of white wine.

Matt's Mom's Tartar Sauce

If tartar sauce is so easy, how come people who can tie their shoes and count to a hundred by tens can't seem to consistently make it dance on their tongues?

Even when sealed and refrigerated, tartar sauce is best and safest when used within two or three days.

MAKES 6 TO 8 SERVINGS

1 cup finely chopped dill pickles

1 cup finely chopped white onions

3 tablespoons finely chopped parsley

juice of 1 lemon

2 cups mayonnaise

Drain the pickles in a strainer or pat them dry with paper towels. Mix all ingredients together in a bowl. Refrigerate until using.

SERVING SUGGESTION
Sprinkle paprika over the sauce for color.

Big Dog Tartar Sauce

When you're having friends over and you want to impress the big dogs with something fancy, this sauce works wonders on broiled or baked fish.

1 cup finely chopped dill pickles

1 cup finely chopped white onions

2 finely chopped hard-boiled eggs

1 tablespoon olive oil

1 tablespoon red wine vinegar

juice of 1 lemon

$^1/_2$ teaspoon Worcestershire sauce

1 teaspoon sugar

Drain the pickles in a drainer or pat them dry with paper towels. Mix all the ingredients in a serving bowl. Refrigerate the sauce in the serving bowl until you're ready to use it, but use right away.

COOKING SUGGESTION
Sprinkle some paprika and mix in finely chopped parsley for a tad more taste.

Big Batch o' BBQ Sauce

We feature this sauce on our barbecue lunches at No Place. It's for big heapings.

I usually put my sauce in a smoker for 2 to 3 hours after it's prepared. I never use liquid smoke as a substitute, and I hope you don't either.

This is more of a Central/South Texas sauce. Farther north toward Dallas and East Texas, the sauces tend to be a little sweeter.

MAKES 40 TO 50 SERVINGS

1 cup white cider vinegar

1 cup Worcestershire sauce

½ cup packed brown sugar

½ cup prepared mustard

1 6-ounce can chipotle peppers

2 cups coarsely chopped white onions

¼ cup chopped garlic

5 cups coarsely chopped fresh tomatoes

2½ cups water

2 bay leaves

1 gallon ketchup

3 tablespoons salt

2 teaspoons pepper

Combine all the ingredients except the ketchup in a large pot and simmer for 30 minutes. Add the ketchup and simmer 30 more minutes.

Pour through a strainer to rid the sauce of the pulp, mashing in the chipotle and tomatoes. Whatever goes through the sieve is ready for use.

COOKING SUGGESTION
After preparing, place in a smoker for 2 to 3 hours for the ultimate flavor.

Cheese Gravy

Cheese Gravy is great on toast, scrambled eggs, rice, biscuits, and mashed potatoes. I'm here to testify, it's good.

2 slices bacon

2 tablespoons flour

2 cups milk

1½ cups grated American cheese

salt and pepper to taste

In your favorite skillet, fry the bacon until it's crispy. Remove it, give it a while to cool down, then crumble the bacon on the side.

Reserve 2 tablespoons of drippings in the skillet. Add the flour and cook on medium heat 1 to 2 minutes. Add the milk and whisk until smooth on medium heat, then turn to low. Add the cheese. It's ready when the cheese melts.

Add salt and pepper to taste. Serve with the crumbled bacon on the side.

Jalapeño Pepper Jelly

Here's yet another dear friend aimed at the center of your dear ol' soul. It's lip-smackin' with barbecued or grilled dishes.

MAKES 8 TO 10 SERVINGS

½ cup pickled jalapeño peppers, minced and seeded

1 cup green bell peppers, minced and seeded

1½ cups apple cider vinegar

5½ cups sugar

6 ounces liquid pectin

green food color

Blend the jalapeño and bell peppers and only a ½ cup of the apple cider vinegar until smooth. Pour the mixture into a large saucepan.

Rinse the blender with the remaining vinegar and add it to the peppers. Stir in the sugar.

Bring the mixture to a boil that cannot be stirred down, then remove it from the heat. Carefully skim the foam off the top, trying not to take out any jalapeños.

Stir in the liquid pectin and green food color. (You can use 2 3-ounce pouches liquid pectin.) Cool for approximately 5 minutes. Pour into sterile jars and seal.

Chipotle Pepper Jelly

Everybody's got his or her own preferences when it comes to toppings. Perhaps you've noticed that some of us are like Marilyn Monroe. We like it hot!

½ cup chipotle peppers, minced and seeded

1 cup green bell peppers, minced and seeded

1½ cups apple cider vinegar

5½ cups sugar

6 ounces liquid pectin

green food color

Blend the chipotle and bell peppers and only a ½ cup of the apple cider vinegar until smooth. Pour the mixture into a large saucepan.

Rinse the blender with the remaining vinegar and add it to the peppers. Stir in the sugar.

Bring the mixture to a boil that cannot be stirred down, then remove it from the heat. Carefully skim the foam off the top, trying not to take out any peppers.

Stir in the liquid pectin and green food color. (You can use 2 3-ounce pouches liquid pectin.) Cool for approximately 5 minutes. Pour into sterile jars and seal.

Mesa Redondo Gravy

This gravy highlights green chiles and jalapeños, which means that the average tenderfoot best have a glass of ice water nearby. The recipe creates an ample supply, but leftovers keep great in the refrigerator.

MAKES 15 TO 20 SERVINGS

12 ounces bacon

1 pound pork sausage

1 pound ground beef or venison

3 tablespoons flour

2 to 3 cloves garlic, chopped

2 4-ounce cans diced green chiles

2 to 4 tablespoons diced jalapeños (depending on how hot you like it)

3 cups milk

kosher salt to taste

black pepper to taste

Cut the bacon crosswise in strips and cook it in a skillet until crisp. Remove each piece with a slotted spoon and reserve the bacon.

In the same skillet, cook the sausage in the bacon drippings until done. Again, remove with a slotted spoon and reserve.

In the same skillet, brown the ground beef or venison, then remove it and reserve.

Reserve 3 tablespoons of grease in the skillet. Add the flour to make a roux, and then add the garlic, chiles, and jalapeños.

Sauté for 5 to 10 minutes while gradually stirring in the milk to the consistency you desire for gravy. Stir occasionally.

Add salt and pepper to taste.

Add all the reserved meat to the skillet and cook until the meat is hot.

SERVING SUGGESTION

For a great breakfast, serve Mesa Redondo Gravy over biscuits. Or, any time of day, serve over rice, rolled in a warm flour tortilla, or over eggs, omelets, or plain ol' toast.

Green Chile/Jalapeño Sauce with Pork

This sauce sings its own harmonies on eggs or over rice or pasta.

2 4-ounce cans diced green chiles

1 4-ounce can diced jalapeños

2 teaspoons Mexican oregano, dried

6 to 8 cloves fresh garlic, peeled and slightly crushed

1 small to medium coarsely chopped onion

3 cups water

2 to 3 teaspoons oil of your choice or bacon grease

2 pounds cubed pork

2 tablespoons flour

1 teaspoon kosher salt

1 cup chicken broth (or additional cup of water)

In a skillet, combine the green chiles, jalapeños, oregano, garlic, onion, and 3 cups of water. Bring to a light boil for approximately 5 minutes.

Reduce the heat and simmer uncovered for 30 minutes, stirring occasionally. When it's slightly thick, pour the sauce into a blender to cool.

Sauté the pork cubes in the skillet with the oil or bacon grease. When brown, remove the pork with a slotted spoon and reserve it.

Remove all but 2 tablespoons of grease from the pan. Add the flour and lightly brown to make a roux.

Add the salt to the sauce in the blender and puree. Add all the sauce in the blender to the roux.

Add the chicken broth (or 1 more cup of water) to achieve the consistency you prefer. Bring the sauce to a light simmer. Add the pork and cook over a light simmer until the pork is tender, approximately 30 minutes to 1 hour.

Matt's Anchovy Hollandaise Sauce

All over Europe, you'll be hard-pressed to find somebody who doesn't like anchovies. Down here in the South and Southwest of the United States, people just think they don't like 'em.

Hollandaise has its own horror stories because of its inclination to curl up and lump. Make your hollandaise this way a couple of times, and you'll be just fine. The little ol' easy techniques can be hard to beat.

MAKES 4 TO 6 SERVINGS

4 rolled anchovies with capers, minced

1 teaspoon anchovy oil

1 stick butter

3 egg yolks

2 teaspoons lemon juice

1 teaspoon dry mustard

pinch of white pepper

Sauté the anchovies and capers in the anchovy oil and butter for 3 to 4 minutes over low heat.

Strain the mixture into a bowl, using the back of a spoon to press gently and drain out all the butter, being careful not to run the anchovies and capers through the sieve.

In a separate bowl, whisk the egg yolks, lemon juice, dry mustard, and white pepper.

Pour yolk mixture into the top of a double boiler and very lightly simmer. Whisk 6 to 8 times, then add the anchovy mixture and whisk until thick.

Serve immediately.

SERVING SUGGESTION
This is great with grilled cheese sandwiches. See my Hollandaise Grilled Cheese (p. 79).

Matt's Hollandaise Sauce No.1

When you want to accent your eggs or vegetables but aren't trying to hit your guests over the head with your own magnificence in the kitchen, here's a good ol' everyday hollandaise sauce.

MAKES 4 TO 6 SERVINGS

1 stick butter

3 egg yolks

2 tablespoons lemon juice

1/4 teaspoon dry mustard

pinch of white pepper

salt to taste

In a double boiler, bring the water to a boil. Add butter to the top boiler, and turn down the heat to a simmer while allowing the butter to melt.

Pour the melted butter into a small bowl and set it aside.

Remove the top boiler from the heat and add the egg yolks, lemon juice, dry mustard, and white pepper. Whisk this mixture until smooth.

Return it to the top boiler to heat, and gradually add butter while continuing to whisk the sauce until it is thick.

Add salt to taste, and serve.

Matt's Hot & Spicy Hollandaise Sauce

This is my favorite sauce for grilled, baked, or poached fish. It works pretty good on omelets, too.

1 stick butter

2 tablespoons chopped jalapeño or serraño peppers

2 tablespoons coarsely chopped onions

2 cloves garlic, thinly sliced

3 egg yolks

2 tablespoons lemon juice

1/4 teaspoon dry mustard

pinch of white pepper

salt to taste

In a small skillet, gently simmer the butter, peppers, onions, and garlic until the onions are translucent.

Strain the mixture into a bowl, pressing gently with the back of a spoon to drain out all butter, but be careful not to run the vegetables through the sieve.

In a separate bowl, whisk the egg yolks, lemon juice, dry mustard, and white pepper.

Pour the egg mixture into the top of a double boiler and continue to whisk 6 to 8 more times. Gradually add the flavored butter.

Add salt to taste, and serve.

Matt's Chipotle Hollandaise Sauce

I've never been all that big on chicken breasts, but this sauce goes great on chicken. It ain't too shabby on catfish either, garnished with some good, fresh cilantro.

MAKES 4 TO 6 SERVINGS

1 stick butter

1 minced chipotle pepper

2 cloves garlic, thinly sliced

3 egg yolks

2 tablespoons lemon juice

1 tablespoon adobo sauce

1/4 teaspoon dry mustard

pinch of white pepper

salt to taste

In a small skillet on low heat, simmer the butter, chipotle peppers, and garlic for 2 minutes. Strain the mixture into a bowl, pressing gently with the back of a spoon to drain all the butter without losing the peppers or garlic.

In a separate bowl, whisk the egg yolks, lemon juice, adobo sauce, dry mustard, and white pepper until the mixture is smooth.

Pour the mixture into the top of a lightly simmering double boiler. After 6 to 8 good whisks, gently add the flavored butter.

Add salt to taste, and serve.

Matt's Thousand Island Dressing

Try this sauce over lettuce wedges or sliced beefsteak tomatoes. It'll make your heart go pitter-pat like it does when you're looking at a river, like the Ol' Rio Grande.

MAKES 6 TO 8 SERVINGS

2 cups mayonnaise

¼ cup ketchup

2 tablespoons Louisiana hot sauce

2 tablespoons finely chopped onions

2 tablespoons finely chopped bell peppers

2 finely chopped hard-boiled eggs

1 teaspoon vinegar

1 teaspoon sugar

½ teaspoon paprika

In a bowl, thoroughly mix all the ingredients. Voila.

Matt's French Dressing

Here's a slight deviation from your everyday French dressing. I tried to steal my mom's recipe, but she makes French dressing differently every time, kind of like the way I sign my name. Nobody's going to copy me or Mom.

MAKES 6 SERVINGS

2 cloves garlic, finely chopped

½ cup vinegar

1½ cups olive oil

¾ teaspoon salt

½ teaspoon white pepper

½ teaspoon dry mustard

1 teaspoon sugar

¾ teaspoon paprika

1 teaspoon chipotle paste
  (optional)

In a mixing bowl, crush the garlic with the back of a spoon, mashing it thoroughly. Add the remaining ingredients and whisk thoroughly.

I recommend adding the Chipotle Paste (see p. 124). It makes the dressing a little spicy and very special. Mix well before serving.

Marco's Chipotle Sour Cream Sauce

My son Marco concocted these next two sour cream sauces for fish, chicken, and vegetables. They're very simple and delicious. Simple things always make great things better.

MAKES 6 SERVINGS

2 cups sour cream

2 chipotle peppers

1 tablespoon adobo sauce

1½ teaspoons lime juice

1 teaspoon sugar

1 teaspoon garlic, minced

3 tablespoons dry white wine

Place all the ingredients in a blender and chop for 15 to 30 seconds, or until the chipotle peppers are chopped fine.

Use this sauce right away.

Marco's No.1 Sour Cream Sauce

This is just a tad different from the previous sour cream sauce. It's all a matter of what makes your taste buds dance.

MAKES 6 SERVINGS

2 cups of sour cream

1½ teaspoons lime juice

1 teaspoon sugar

½ fresh, seeded jalapeño pepper

½ teaspoon chopped fresh garlic or a small clove of garlic

3 tablespoons dry white wine

Place all the ingredients in a blender and chop for 15 to 30 seconds.

SERVING SUGGESTION
Serve over grilled or baked chicken and fish.

Hot Chipotle
Barbecue Sauce

I like this sauce over grilled catfish and chicken, or as a dip for fried fish. It will also give your beans more life. If you use it in refried beans, go with 1 tablespoon of sauce per 2 cups of refrieds.

MAKES 3 1/2 CUPS

3 tablespoons Worcestershire sauce

3 tablespoons brown sugar

3 tablespoons white vinegar

2 cups ketchup

2 cups coarsely chopped tomatoes

1½ teaspoons prepared mustard

2 large garlic cloves, crushed

1 small bay leaf or ½ large bay leaf

½ teaspoon salt

¼ teaspoon black pepper

1 7-ounce can chipotle peppers in adobo sauce

1 cup water

Place all the ingredients in a saucepan and bring to a boil over high heat. Turn to a simmer for 30 minutes. Turn off heat and let cool for 30 minutes.

Remove the bay leaf. Place everything else into a blender and blend until smooth. Pour into a sieve to remove all the seeds and pulp. The sauce that makes it through the sieve is ready to eat.

Giblet Gravy for Goose and Wild Turkey

This is a hunter's gravy, and when I think about hunting I think about camouflage, and when I think about camouflage I recall this story.

I was maybe 13 when I escaped from the house early one evening to go hunting at a nearby creek in South Austin. I bagged four plump sparrows with my BB gun and got dirtier than necessary in the process.

I knew Granny Gaytan would not be pleased if she found out I was AWOL, so I intended to wash off at the hydrant on the side of the house and get back to my room as soon as possible. Before I could grab the hose, Granny came wandering out the back door.

It was dusk, and luckily she didn't spot me. I quietly slid the sparrows and my rifle under a bush and gently laid down right into a mud puddle in the middle of our dirt driveway.

I kept waiting for Granny to leave so I could rinse off, but she was in no rush.

I looked up the road and here came Meliton Torres, our neighbor, in his automobile.

Mr. Torres turned right into our driveway. To keep from getting run over, I jumped straight up and scared the living daylights out of him. It must have looked like the creature from the black lagoon.

Granny grabbed me and popped me on the head with her broom, which she carried around as if she used it for transportation.

If I had it to do all over again, I'd have let Mr. Torres run me over. It would have been a lot less painful.

Fortunately, even when I was bad, Granny still fed me real good. Before too long, I settled down in front of a beautifully cooked bird with giblet gravy.

This gravy is very good with dove giblets, but take care not to use wormy little dove necks. You must use 6 to 8 doves to make a good gravy.

I do not recommend using liver; it may be too strong for some.

Keep in mind that you are making this gravy from the turkey or birds that you are cooking at the time.

MAKES 4 TO 6 SERVINGS

giblets and necks from birds

2 tablespoons butter

2 tablespoons finely chopped
white onions (optional)

$^1/_2$ cup finely chopped
mushrooms (optional)

2 cups chicken stock (see p. 44)

$^1/_2$ cup water

2 tablespoons cornstarch

$^1/_2$ cup half-and-half or heavy
cream

salt and pepper to taste

Sauté the birds' giblets and necks in butter over low heat until lightly brown. If desired, add the onions and mushrooms.

Add the stock and gently simmer for $2^1/_2$ to 3 hours. Add water as you go, maintaining the same level throughout.

When the bird you are cooking is almost done and you're ready for the gravy, remove the giblets and necks from the stock. Scrape as much meat from the necks as possible, which may not be much. Chop the giblets. Return the neck meat and giblets to the stock.

Mix the cornstarch with the water and add it to the simmering broth. When thickened, turn to a very low heat and add the half-and-half or cream. Simmer gently.

Add salt and pepper to taste.

SERVING SUGGESTION
When your bird's ready, pour the gravy over it and chow down.

CHAPTER SIX

Breads

To me, breads should not jump up and down clamoring for attention. They've got their place on any plate and in many bowls, but good breads are willing to allow the entrees and side dishes to take center stage.

Just like you don't need a bunch of spicy side dishes with a spicy main course, you want your breads to balance things out, maybe give your taste buds a break. If your main course has some kick, go with a gentler bread. But, if your main course is on the mild side, try a bread with some spunk.

While going from state to state and on down into Mexico during my travels, I found that bread recipes have little variation.

The best ones are basic, often with the same ingredients. Techniques do vary a little. My favorite involves using a pre-heated skillet *inside* a preheated oven. That particular method makes a huge difference to me.

The skillet is my sniping tool. It allows me to hit any appetite at any distance.

Matt's Favorite Biscuits

When it comes to making my favorite biscuits, you will need to use your favorite 10-inch oven-proof skillet, preferably cast-iron. It's the best cooking vessel in the history of the open fire and in modern kitchens to boot. My most prized possession is my ol' 10-inch, cast-iron skillet.

MAKES 8 BISCUITS

2 cups flour

2 teaspoons baking powder

2 teaspoons sugar

$1/4$ cup lard or shortening (Crisco works best)

1 fresh egg

$1/3$ cup milk

1 tablespoon butter

Place your skillet inside the oven and preheat the oven to 475° for 15 to 18 minutes.

Mix the flour, baking powder, and sugar, and blend in a bowl. Add the lard or shortening, and work the mixture together with warm hands.

Mix the egg and milk together first, then add to the mixture slowly, continuing to hand blend. The mix may feel a little wet, but that is what you want.

Make a ball and pinch it in half, forming 2 balls. Pinch each in half again. Now you have 4 balls. Pinch each of them so you have 8 balls. The balls will be a little larger in size than a golf ball. Flatten the balls to be about a $1/2$-inch thick.

Remove the skillet from the oven. Add the butter to the skillet on low heat and let it melt.

Place the flattened biscuits in the skillet. It should be a little crowded and tight, which is just right.

Cook for 15 to 18 minutes at 475°, or until golden brown.

Beer Biscuits

Whether your favorite beer is light or full, domestic or foreign (meaning anything that isn't Lone Star), you'll like these biscuits with durn near anything. I'd eat 'em like popcorn if my belly would allow.

MAKES 8 BISCUITS

2 cups flour

2 teaspoons baking powder

2 teaspoons sugar

1/4 cup lard or shortening (Crisco works best)

1 fresh egg

1 tablespoon heavy cream

1/4 cup beer of your choice

3/4 cup shredded sharp Cheddar cheese

1 tablespoon butter

Place a 10-inch oven-proof skillet in the oven at 475° and preheat for 15 to 18 minutes.

Mix the flour, baking powder, and sugar, and blend it all together.

Add the lard or shortening, and work the dough together with warm hands.

Mix the egg, heavy cream, and beer together, and add it to the mixture, continuing to hand blend. The mix may feel a little wet—that's what you want.

Make a ball and pinch it in half, giving you 2 balls. Pinch each in half again. Now you have 4 balls. Pinch those in half for 8 balls. The balls will be a little larger in size than a golf ball. Flatten the balls a little, making them about a 1/2-inch thick.

Remove the skillet from the oven. Add the butter to the skillet and let it melt on low heat.

Place the flattened biscuits in the skillet. It should be a little crowded, which is how you want it.

Cook for 15 to 18 minutes at 475°, or until golden brown.

Pan Loco

Do not fear if these biscuits look dry and crumbly; that's their nature. They still taste mighty fine.

MAKES 8 BISCUITS

¼ cup lard or shortening
  (Crisco works best)

2 cups flour

2 tablespoons baking powder

¾ teaspoon salt

⅓ cup hot water

1 additional tablespoon
  shortening

Preheat the oven to 475° for 15 to 18 minutes with your favorite 10-inch oven-proof skillet inside. You can also use a 9-inch square pan or cookie sheet, instead of a skillet.

In a bowl, mix the ¼ cup of lard or shortening with the flour. When the mixture is very crumbly, thoroughly mix in all the other ingredients except the final tablespoon of shortening.

Form one big ball and then separate into 8 even balls by pinching each in half.

Add the tablespoon of shortening to the hot skillet.

Flatten the 8 balls into ½-inch balls and place them into the skillet.

In a 475° oven, cook 15 to 18 minutes, or until golden brown.

Flour Tortillas

Few items ever come as handy as a flour tortilla. You can put almost anything in one.

¼ cup lard or shortening
  (Crisco works best)

2 cups flour

2 tablespoons baking powder

¾ teaspoon salt

⅓ cup hot water

1 additional tablespoon
  shortening

Mix the lard or shortening with the flour. When the mixture is very crumbly, add all the other ingredients except the final tablespoon of shortening. Mix well.

Make one ball and continue to divide in half until you have 16 balls. They should be smaller in size than golf balls. Cover the balls with a towel, and let them rest for 30 to 40 minutes in a warm spot.

When ready, dust a rolling pin and the surface with flour.

Heat a cooking grill or a large skillet and start rolling each ball of dough as thinly as possible.

Place the dough onto the cooking vessel. When the tortilla starts to bubble, flip it over. Keep an eye on them; you'll know when they reach the texture you desire.

Place the cooked tortillas in a basket to keep warm.

Continue this process until all the tortillas are done.

Cornbread

There'll always be a soft spot in my heart for good ol' fashioned cornbread.

1¹/₂ cups cornmeal

¹/₂ cup flour

2 teaspoons baking powder

³/₄ teaspoon salt

1 tablespoon sugar (optional)

¹/₄ cup shortening

1 egg

1 cup milk

1 additional tablespoon shortening

Combine all the dry ingredients, and add the ¹/₄ cup of shortening. Hand blend until thoroughly mixed and crumbly.

Mix the egg and milk together first, then add to the dry ingredients.

Preheat the oven to 450° with your favorite 10-inch oven-proof skillet inside. When the oven is pre-heated, remove the skillet and add the tablespoon of shortening to the skillet.

Once the shortening melts, add the batter to the skillet and cook in the oven for 35 to 40 minutes, until lightly brown. The cornbread should spring back when you touch it.

Chipotle Cornbread

I usually prefer my cornbread with an attitude when my main dish is easygoing and not overly spicy.

MAKES 4 TO 6 SERVINGS

1½ cups cornmeal

½ cup flour

2 teaspoons baking powder

¾ teaspoon salt

1 tablespoon sugar (optional)

¼ cup shortening

2 whole chipotle peppers in adobo sauce

1 egg

1 cup milk

1 additional tablespoon shortening

Combine all the dry ingredients.

Add the ¼ cup of shortening.

Using a blender, blend the chipotle peppers using 1 tablespoon of the adobo sauce, egg, and milk. Blend until the chipotle is chopped real fine. Add to the dry ingredients once they are thoroughly mixed and crumbly.

Preheat the oven to 450° with your favorite 10-inch oven-proof skillet inside. When the oven is ready, remove the skillet and add the tablespoon of shortening to the skillet.

Once the shortening melts, add the batter to the skillet and cook in the oven for 35 to 40 minutes until lightly brown. When you touch the cornbread and it springs back, it's ready.

Beer Cornbread

This is a kissing cousin of the aforementioned Beer Biscuits.

1¹/₂ cups cornmeal

¹/₂ cup flour

2 teaspoons baking powder

³/₄ teaspoon salt

1 tablespoon sugar (optional)

¹/₄ cup shortening

1 egg

1¹/₂ cups your favorite beer

2 tablespoons heavy cream

1 cup grated sharp Cheddar cheese

1 additional tablespoon shortening

Combine all the dry ingredients. Add the ¹/₄ cup of shortening.

Mix the egg, beer, cream, and cheese together and add to the dry ingredients once they are thoroughly mixed and crumbly.

Preheat the oven to 450° with your favorite 10-inch oven-proof skillet inside. When the oven is pre-heated, remove the skillet and add tablespoon of shortening.

Once the shortening melts, add the batter to the skillet and cook in the oven for 35 to 40 minutes until lightly brown. When the cornbread springs back when you touch it, it's ready.

Hush Puppies

Hush puppies are a Southern delight. It never hurts to say "ya'll" several times while fixing these.

MAKES 4 TO 6 SERVINGS

1½ cups cornmeal

½ cup flour

¾ teaspoon salt

¼ cup shortening

1 egg

1 cup milk

½ cup minced onions

¼ cup finely minced jalapeños, drained and seeded

oil for deep frying

Combine all the dry ingredients, then add ¼ cup of shortening.

Mix the egg, milk, onions, and jalapeños together and add this mixture to the dry ingredients once they are thoroughly mixed and crumbly.

Heat the oil in a skillet or deep fat fryer. The oil is hot and ready when you sprinkle in water and it pops.

Put the batter into the hot grease one spoonful at a time. Fry until crispy.

The hush puppies will not be round. They will be fat and crisp.

Plain Gorditas

Here's the original Mexican cornbread, dating back to the Aztecs. I ate my weight in these when I was little, and they're finally beginning to show.

oil or grease (¹⁄₄-inch deep in your skillet)

¹⁄₄ cup lard or shortening

2 cups dry masa for making tortillas

1 cup water

salt to taste

Add enough oil or grease to fill your favorite skillet ¹⁄₄-inch deep.

Mix the lard or shortening and the dry masa until they are thoroughly combined. Add the water and knead well, then form 16 little balls.

Flatten the balls in the palms of your hands to approximately ¹⁄₄-inch thick. Drop into the hot oil or grease and brown on both sides.

Drain on paper towels. Keep them warm by wrapping them in a cloth.

Salt the gorditas before eating.

SERVING SUGGESTION

These are good for dipping in queso and guacamole, or to eat with beans or stews.

Indian Fried Bread

Perhaps you've got your own favorite Indian bread toppings. I like mine with maple syrup, butter, and powdered sugar.

2 cups flour

2 teaspoons baking powder

2 teaspoons sugar

1/4 cup lard or shortening (Crisco works best)

1 egg

1/3 cup milk

oil or grease (1-inch deep in the bottom of your skillet)

Mix all the dry ingredients and blend.

Add the shortening and work together with warm hands.

Mix the egg and milk and add to the mixture, continuing to hand blend. The mix may feel a little wet, but that is what you want.

Make a ball and pinch in half. Now you have 2 balls. Pinch in half again. Now you have 4 balls. Continue balling until you have 8 balls. The balls will be a little larger in size than a golf ball. Flatten the balls a little, making them about a 1/2-inch thick.

Punch a hole in the center of each ball with your finger. This is to allow the grease to run through, avoiding a doughy center.

Heat your favorite 10-inch skillet about an inch deep with grease. Place the balls in the skillet, trying not to crowd. Fry to a golden brown.

Spicy Gorditas

I enjoy these with beans. Gorditas are also an excellent appetizer.

It's best to mix these spicy ones with a spoon, or wear plastic gloves because the chipotle peppers might otherwise burn your hands.

MAKES 4 TO 6 SERVINGS

2 whole chipotle peppers

$1/4$ cup lard or shortening

2 cups corn flour for making tortillas

2 tablespoons chili powder

1 cup water

2 tablespoons adobo sauce

oil or grease ($1/4$-inch deep in a skillet)

salt to taste

Chop the chipotle peppers very fine.

Mix the lard or shortening, the corn flour, and the chili powder until they are thoroughly combined. Add the chopped peppers, water, and 2 tablespoons of adobo sauce and knead well, then form 16 little balls.

Flatten the balls in the palms of your hands to approximately $1/4$-inch thick. Deep-fry in $1/4$-inch hot grease, turning and browning on both sides.

Drain on paper towels. Keep them warm by wrapping them in a cloth.

Salt the gorditas before eating.

CHAPTER SEVEN

Drinks and Desserts

I'VE NEVER POSSESSED MUCH OF a sweet tooth, but I have included several desserts just to keep the rest of you happy.

On the other hand, when it comes to a good coffee drink, cognac, or bourbon following dinner, I'll be among the first to have my hand up.

There's nothing better than a campfire, a good cigar, an after-dinner drink, and some warm eyes batting back at me across the fire.

I can't get my dog Peanutty to bat his eyes worth a darn. He can squint, but he can't bat. My wife Estella, however, is a master batter.

You'll find a few recipes in this section that might cause you to bat your eyes a little more freely as well.

DRINKS

This was my favorite section of the entire book when it came to testing recipes. I've tested, retested, and tested again—sometimes for decades.

But I've tried not to overdo it. My palate cleanser for testing drinks is a little straight Jack Daniel's. It cleans the cobwebs from my tongue and encourages a sensitivity to my testing. As long as I don't test too many items in a day.

Longhorn Margarita

Hailing from Austin, we break out the Longhorn Margaritas after every University of Texas victory. Or whenever we can come up with a good excuse.

MAKES 4 SERVINGS

1 quart orange juice, freshly squeezed or store-bought

6 shots tequila (Sauza White works best for me)

juice of 1 fresh lime or 1 lemon (about 2 tablespoons)

3 shots Cointreau or Grand Marnier

ice

In a pitcher, mix the orange juice, tequila, lime or lemon juice, and the Cointreau or Grand Marnier.

Fill your drinking glasses with crushed ice, and pour the drink over the ice.

SERVING SUGGESTION

To make each drink really festive, mix $1/4$ teaspoon cayenne pepper and 1 package presweetened Orange Kool-Aid with the juice from one lime. Rim the glasses in the Kool-Aid mix. It sounds hokey, but it makes me happy.

Pick-Up Proof Margarita Rim

Early in the season when hunters head for the deer leases, we like to ride around in our trucks and jeeps with a margarita or two. The most embarrassing predicament is to draw the black bean and have to be the driver because he can't partake.

When on the road, it's advisable to have some back-up rimmed cups. We solve this problem by rimming 10 Styrofoam cups with honey and salt, all at once. The honey keeps the salt on the cups. Even out of Styrofoam a margarita tastes good, but it's not advisable to make too many at once when red ants are around.

MAKES 8 TO 12 SALT-RIMMED CUPS

¼ cup pure honey

¼ teaspoon cayenne pepper

¼ cup rock salt

Blend the honey and cayenne together, then stick in a microwave for 30 seconds on a large round plate. On a separate plate, spread around a quarter cup of rock salt, medium grind. Dip your Styrofoam cup in the honey, then let it sit for a minute.

When ready for a drink, turn the cup down onto the rock salt (it'll stay on your cup even on the roughest roads).

DRINKS AND DESSERTS • 163

Arkansas Margarita

I was doing some serious scientific research one day while hanging around with some fine representatives of Arkansas, as we sat on a riverbank fishing.

We began discussing the various rims I do for margaritas. They started smiling, and the way they were smiling I know if I'd heard a banjo in the background I'd have made a run for it.

We got around to making one of their favorite drinks that includes a rim. White lightning may be hard to come by in a liquor store near you, but it's always available in the hills of Arkansas. Servings depend on the size of your hands, but I promise this will make all you can stand. Cooking aside: I'm embarrassed to say the same thing happened to me on the banks of the San Gabriel River in Texas, when again our conversation came to drinking and margaritas and whatnot. We basically came up with the same recipe, only these guys were from Oklahoma.

MAKES ALL YOU CAN STAND

paper cup (Styrofoam is hard to come by in Arkansas)

hog lard or drippings, in the bottom of a skillet

handful or two of crushed pork rinds or pork skins

some buttermilk at room temperature

bootleg whiskey from Arkansas (a.k.a. white lightning)

Dip the cup in the hog lard, then roll it in the pork rinds to get a good crust on the rim. Mix the buttermilk and white lightning half-and-half. Let it sit for a minute or two so that the clabber from the buttermilk will rise.

Slowly sip the clabber, running your tongue over the hog lard and pork rinds.

It takes a little getting used to, but as soon as you get to the white lightning, shoot it.

Margarita Mix No.2

My favorite margaritas are on the rocks, but it's so difficult for most people to come up with the perfect formula because some prefer a sweeter taste while others like a tart mix.

I came up with a mix that should make everybody happy. Hopefully, it'll put a halt to all the bellyaching. In case anybody does complain, send 'em to me.

MAKES 6 DRINKS

1 cup fresh lime juice

$^1/_2$ cup sugar

$^1/_2$ cup Cointreau

1 bottle tequila (Sauza White preferred)

1 lime, wedged

In a quart container, add the lime juice, sugar, and Cointreau, and shake well. Fill to the top with water and shake some more.

Rim a glass with salt, and fill with ice. Add 1 part tequila to 3 parts mix. Serve with large wedges of lime, in case someone wants a tarter drink.

Margarita Mix No.3

Our taste tests show this No. 3 mix appeals more to women, while men seem to lean (and I do mean lean) toward No. 2. Don't ask me why. It's simply worked out that way.

MAKES 6 DRINKS

$^1/_2$ cup fresh lemon juice

$^1/_2$ cup fresh lime juice

$^1/_2$ cup sugar

$^1/_2$ cup Grand Marnier

1 bottle tequila (Sauza White preferred)

In a quart container, add the lemon, lime, sugar, and Grand Marnier and shake well. Fill to the top with water and shake again.

Rim a glass with salt and fill with ice. Use 3 parts of the mix to every 1 part tequila per glass. Drink up, at your own pace, of course.

Pumpkin Eggnog

Several years ago, I was asked to participate in San Antonio's Nutcracker Ball—a gala charity event that raises money for battered women.

I didn't realize all these fancy chefs were going to be there, too. They were rarin' to go with all their fancy equipment, and I was more than a little intimidated.

So I found the nearest grocery store and purchased some nutmeg, cayenne, cinnamon, powdered sugar, and canned pumpkin. Then I dropped by a liquor store for a bottle of Presidente Brandy and another of peppermint schnapps.

I borrowed a can opener from a bellhop and went to work. I grabbed some champagne glasses and dipped the lips into the peppermint schnapps, then into the powdered sugar.

I filled the glasses with icy cold eggnog mixed with pumpkin and lots of brandy, and everybody just went crazy over that Pumpkin Eggnog.

A few of the other chefs cornered me later in the evening and asked me what was the secret to my eggnog.

"Well," I said, "I cooked my eggs in a double-boiler with a little milk. Not too much milk, just a little. Then I chilled it. I baked the pumpkin at 225° for four hours, then mashed it, cooled it, and swirled it.

"I let it sit for twenty-four hours, and when I reached San Antonio, I chilled my brandy before mixing four parts eggnog to one part brandy. Served it with a seasoned rim."

I was fibbing, of course, but it just sounded better than telling them I opened up a cardboard box of eggnog and some ol' rusty can and mixed 'em all up.

MAKES 6 TO 8 DRINKS

1 gallon of the eggnog of your choice

1 can prepared pumpkin

1 teaspoon cinnamon

$^{1}/_{2}$ teaspoon cayenne

1 tablespoon crumbled brown sugar

brandy or bourbon of your choice (as much as you like)

peppermint schnapps

1 cup powdered sugar

Thoroughly combine all ingredients except the peppermint schnapps and powdered sugar.

Rim the glass with the peppermint schnapps and dip in the powdered sugar.

SERVING SUGGESTION

Another variation is to use one box of frozen strawberries with syrup instead of the pumpkin, and puree in the eggnog. Jack Daniel's whiskey is a delicious addition to this holiday treat.

What Goes Around, Comes Around Banana Eggnog with Dark Rum

This is primarily the same recipe as the previous Pumpkin Eggnog, but I've got another story in me and wish to tell it here.

I can't remember when or where I heard this one, but eggnog reminds me of Christmas so it must have been during the holidays.

This young boy lived in a little town in the Texas Panhandle not far from the New Mexico borderline, and he was depressed because everybody in his family had a present for their mom except him.

It snowed and sleeted the night before, and he was walking dejectedly down a sidewalk when he spotted a dime glistening in the snow.

He took the dime to the town square and ducked into a store and asked what he could purchase. "Not much," came the answer. So he went to the next store and got the same reply.

He walked into a flower shop and asked the old man at the counter, "Can I buy a flower for my momma with this dime?"

The old man stepped into the back and returned with a bouquet of roses, neatly trimmed.

"Sir, I only have a dime," the boy protested.

"We have a sale on flowers today," the old man responded while taking the dime.

As the boy danced down the street toward home, the shop owner's wife came out of the back and said, "Honey, you could have made a handsome sum today off those flowers and now they're gone."

The old man shrugged and said, "The right person came by."

And then he told his wife this story:

"When I was about the age of that little boy, my momma needed a present. An old man gave me $5, and I told him I could never pay him back. He said, 'That's okay, son, someone helped me out one Christmas and I want to do a good deed in return. What goes around, comes around.'

"When that little boy walked in here, I heard that same ol' grizzly voice telling me this is pay-back day. I reckon someday that little boy will carry on the tradition. He'll give a little money to someone who needs it, and he'll hear my grizzly voice in his own head, whispering, 'What goes around, comes around.'"

MAKES 6 TO 8 DRINKS

1 gallon eggnog of your choice

2 cups peeled bananas

1 teaspoon cinnamon

1/2 teaspoon cayenne

1 tablespoon crumbled brown
    sugar

your favorite dark rum (as much
    as you like)

peppermint schnapps

1 cup powdered sugar

Thoroughly mix or blend into the eggnog, the bananas, and all the dry ingredients. Add the dark rum.

Rim the glass with the peppermint schnapps and dip in the powdered sugar.

Rum Coke Float

The following three floats are adult desserts. There's a small child in all of us. When you bring both worlds together, things work out so much better. Here's the taste of your childhood combined with a light, after-dinner buzz.

MAKES 1 FLOAT

1 scoop vanilla ice cream (use good quality ice cream)

1 1/2 ounces rum or to taste

Coca-Cola

wedge of lime

Add the ice cream to a glass.

Add the rum and the Coca-Cola.

Squeeze the lime wedge over the top. Drink up.

Bourbon Coke Float

If you prefer bourbon over rum, try this recipe.

MAKES 1 FLOAT

2 mint leaves

1 scoop vanilla ice cream (use a good quality ice cream)

1 1/2 ounces bourbon or to taste

Coca-Cola

Maraschino cherries with juice

Crush the mint leaves in the bottom of the glass.

Add the ice cream to the glass.

Add the bourbon and then fill it close to the rim with Coca-Cola.

Garnish with a cherry and 1 teaspoon of cherry juice if desired. Drink up.

Brandy Coke Float

Brandy does the trick, too, if bourbon and rum aren't your fancy.

1 scoop vanilla ice cream (use a good quality ice cream)

2 tablespoons chopped fresh or frozen peaches

peach brandy

Coca-Cola

Add the ice cream and peaches to a glass.

Add the brandy and the Coca-Cola.

Garnish with a peach slice. Drink up.

Chocolate Atole

Another lesson learned from Mom: Chocolate Atole is a great pick-me-up in the mornings. It'll really get you cranked up if you've got a hard day ahead and keep you full of energy.

2 cups water

3 ounces Mexican chocolate or ¼ cup Hershey's cocoa powder, mixed with 1 teaspoon cinnamon and 1 teaspoon sugar (to taste)

small piece of cinnamon stick

½ cup dry masa harina (flour)

4 cups milk

1 cup sugar

Put the water, chocolate or cocoa powder, and cinnamon stick in a saucepan, and boil uncovered for 5 minutes over medium heat. Stir regularly to avoid scorching.

On the side, mix the masa harina with 2 cups of milk until it's smooth, then add it to the boiling saucepan. Add the remaining 2 cups of milk and the sugar, and mix until smooth.

Continue to cook over medium heat until it starts to boil.

Reduce the heat and simmer for 2 to 3 minutes, stirring constantly.

This boils over easily, so stay with it.

SERVING SUGGESTION

Serve in a large mug, garnished with whipped cream and a sprinkle of powdered cinnamon. Try it with sweet tamales or buttered toast.

COFFEE DRINKS

Only a couple of years back, dessert menus at finer restaurants listed pretty cakes and pies and other various, traditional dessert dishes.

Today, coffee drinks are the after-dinner craze, and I don't mean choosing between regular and decaf. Coffee drinks have taken our shores, and cups, by storm.

The National Coffee Association reports 113 million Americans drink coffee everyday, and 21 million of those are daily gourmet coffee drinkers.

That got me and my No Place barkeep, Kirk Rogers, to doing a considerable amount of tasting and mixing. We even took a few night courses after closing the restaurant.

There's nothing worse than being drunk and wired at the same time, so we recommend you use decaf for testing purposes.

The Teeth of the Hair of the Dog That Bit You

This is a hangover remedy (not recommended by doctors, but it works for me).

MAKES 1 CUP

2 ounces Presidente brandy

1 BC (aspirin) powder

1 teaspoon brown sugar

1 light sprinkling of cinnamon

coffee of your choice

First, warm a coffee mug in an oven, or with hot water. Mix in the aforementioned ingredients, and add your favorite hot coffee.

Spanish Coffee

MAKES 1 CUP

1¹⁄₄ ounces Licor 43

coffee of your choice

Mix well and top with whipped cream.

Kindred Spirit

MAKES 1 CUP

³⁄₄ ounce Frangelico

³⁄₄ ounce Bailey's Irish Cream

coffee of your choice

Mix well, top with whipped cream, and sip away.

Vanilla Cappuccino

MAKES 1 CUP

³⁄₄ ounce Licor 43

³⁄₄ ounce Godiva Cappuccino
   Liqueur

coffee of your choice

Stir, top with whipped cream, and serve.

Mediterranean Coffee

MAKES 1 CUP

$^1/_2$ ounce Cointreau

$^1/_2$ ounce Tia Maria

$^1/_2$ ounce brandy

coffee of your choice

Rim a warm coffee cup or glass with sugar. Add the liqueur, then fill with coffee. Top with whipped cream.

Puerto Rican Cider

MAKES 1 CUP

$1^1/_4$ ounces Captain Morgan Spice Rum

1 packet instant hot apple cider mix

Pour the liquor and cider mix into a mug or coffee cup, then fill with hot water. Top with whipped cream.

Mexican Coffee

MAKES 1 CUP

$^3/_4$ ounce Kahlua

$^3/_4$ ounce brandy

coffee of your choice

Mix the liqueurs into a warm mug, and fill with coffee. Top with whipped cream.

Tuaca 'Bout It

MAKES 1 CUP

1¼ ounces Tuaca

1 packet instant hot apple cider mix

Put the Tuaca and cider mix in a hot cup or mug and fill with hot water. Stir well, then top with whipped cream.

Damn Hot Chocolate

MAKES 1 CUP

1¼ ounces Hot Damn Cinnamon Schnapps

1 packet instant hot apple cider mix

Mix the schnapps and cider mix in a warm cup or mug and fill with hot water. Stir well, then top with whipped cream.

DESSERTS

In my circle of family and friends, we like to eat so much during dinner that our bellies are actually shiny and wrinkle free. That doesn't leave much room for desserts. We prefer saving desserts for late-night snacking, or with coffee in the mornings and late afternoons.

These desserts conservatively added a good four to five pounds to my belly while I was getting them just right. I mean every calorie raced right to my belly, no place else. It was obvious to my buddies at exactly which point in time I was doing my testing.

Sweet Potato Custard

This was a wintertime delight when I was growing up. It's so homey and comforting, especially since Mom made it this way.

MAKES 6 SERVINGS

1 cup cooked, mashed sweet potatoes or pumpkin (calabaza)

1½ cups milk

½ cup firmly packed brown sugar

½ teaspoon ground cinnamon

½ teaspoon salt

¼ teaspoon ground ginger

¼ teaspoon freshly grated orange zest

3 lightly beaten eggs

Preheat oven to 350°.

In a large bowl, thoroughly mix the sweet potatoes, milk, brown sugar, cinnamon, salt, ginger, and orange zest.

Add the eggs to the bowl, and mix with a spoon until completely smooth.

Fill a roasting pan with 1½ inches hot water.

Pour the custard mix into individual cups, or into a single 9-inch baking dish. Place the cups or dish into a roasting pan and place uncovered in the oven.

Bake individual cups 45 minutes at 350°; or, bake the single baking dish at 350° for 1 hour, or until a knife blade inserted into the center of the custard comes out clean.

Let the custard cool thoroughly, then refrigerate it for 2 to 3 hours.

SERVING SUGGESTION
Serve garnished with a dab of whipped cream and a sprinkle of pecan dust.

Margarita Bars

There's actually no liquor involved in this recipe, but those of you who dabble in margaritas should notice some similarities.

The following five recipes are popular at Matt's Texas Coffee & Mexican Bakery in the Macy's in Dallas. The serving size depends on how you cut them up.

MAKES ONE 9 X 13-INCH JELLY ROLL PAN

FOR THE CRUST:

2 cups softened butter

1 cup powdered sugar

4 cups flour

4 teaspoons lime juice

FOR THE FILLING:

8 eggs well beaten

4 cups sugar

1 teaspoon salt

$3/4$ teaspoon lime juice

2 teaspoons orange extract

2 teaspoons baking powder

3 tablespoons flour

margarita salt or powdered sugar

PREPARING THE CRUST:

Cream the butter and sugar in a mixing bowl. Add the flour and lime juice. Press into a greased 9 x 13-inch jelly roll pan, making sure to cover the bottom and all sides. Bake at 325° for approximately 20 minutes, or until golden brown.

PREPARING THE FILLING:

Combine the eggs and the sugar, then add the remaining ingredients and mix well. Pour the mixture into the crust and bake for approximately 30 minutes, or until the filling has set. Remove from the oven and let cool.

The bars are less sticky if chilled before cutting. They keep well in the freezer.

SERVING SUGGESTION
Sprinkle with margarita salt, powdered sugar, or both.

Peach Jalapeño Bars

Here's another cookie making a name for itself at Macy's. When you cut them up, the size of the cookie bar depends entirely on the size of the mouth it's headed into.

MAKES ONE 9 X 13-INCH COOKIE SHEET

FOR THE CRUST:

3 fresh jalapeños, stems removed, cut in half, do not remove seeds

1¹/₂ cups melted butter

1¹/₂ cups brown sugar

2 cups flour

1 teaspoon baking powder

¹/₂ teaspoon salt

2¹/₂ cups oats

FOR THE TOPPING:

10-ounce jar peach preserves

1 cup chopped pecans

Place the jalapeños in a food processor and pulse until finely chopped.

On the side, combine the butter and brown sugar.

Mix the flour, baking powder, salt, oats, and chopped jalapeños, then add to the butter mixture and stir well. Do not use a mixer.

Spread into a greased 9 x 13-inch cookie sheet and press evenly, using gloves or a spoon.

Bake at 350° for 20 minutes.

Mix together the preserves and pecans. Spread over the crust, and bake for 10 minutes.

Cool and cut into squares.

South of the Border Granola Bars

A few of these granola bars, a sunny day, a good drink, and a señorita will make you sing songs south of the border, no matter what border you're nearest. The serving size depends on how you cut them.

1 to 2 pounds of 1-ounce can oats

1 14-ounce package shredded coconut

2 cups melted butter

2 pounds brown sugar

2 cups maple syrup

1 tablespoon cinnamon

2 cups pecans

2 cups sunflower seeds

3 cups chopped dried mango

3 cups chopped dried papaya

Mix all ingredients in a very big bowl. Your hands work best for this. Mix until thoroughly combined.

Press the mixture into 2 to 3 cookie sheets, packing firmly. Bake at 300° until golden brown, which should be approximately 30 minutes.

While still warm, cut into squares.

Let the bars cool, remove them from the pan, and wrap them individually in plastic or store in an airtight container.

Mexican Wedding Cookies

When Estella and I got married those many moons ago, I was asked to make a bunch of those finger sandwiches filled with tuna and chicken salad for the reception.

I've tried making those things time and time again, and I can never get them to turn out. So I went fishing that morning instead.

The red fish were running so good, I took Estella back the day after the wedding. I thought I was in heaven, sitting there with one arm around a beautiful woman and the other hanging on to a fishing pole, with those red fish biting.

Never mind the finger snacks. You should never get married in Mexico or South Texas without these wedding cookies.

The serving size depends on how large you make the balls of dough.

MAKES ABOUT 6 DOZEN COOKIES

2 cups softened butter

1 cup sugar

4 cups flour

2 cups pecans

1 tablespoon vanilla (Mexican vanilla works best)

2 tablespoons water

2 teaspoons ground cinnamon

powdered sugar

Mix the softened butter with the sugar, and add the remaining ingredients except for the powdered sugar into the butter mixture and mix thoroughly. Shape into balls or crescents.

Bake 35 minutes at 350°.

Cool thoroughly. Roll the cookies into the powdered sugar.

Sweet Dreams Tamales

These aren't the traditional tamales you might be expecting.

To begin with, there's not a tamale in the recipe.

These are sweet and very good, cold or at room temperature. Either way, they're guaranteed to give you a night's worth of sweet dreams.

You can purchase the tamale husks in the produce or Mexican sections of most grocery stores. If you can't find tamales, use corn. Don't foul up and eat the husks; just eat the goodies you put inside.

MAKES ABOUT 2 DOZEN CANDIES

tamale or corn husks (1 per
   candy, about 24)

6 squares of white chocolate
   (1 6-ounce box)

¹/₂ teaspoon vanilla

¹/₂ teaspoon cinnamon

Soak the husks until pliable. Dry off the excess water with a towel, and set the husks aside.

Melt the chocolate according to package directions. Stir in the vanilla and cinnamon. Let the mixture cool for 5 minutes.

Open the husks and, depending on the size of the husk, put 1 to 2 teaspoons of chocolate lengthwise down the middle of the husk. Wrap the husk around the chocolate, and chill in the refrigerator until the chocolate reaches the firmness you desire.

SERVING SUGGESTION
Serve cold or, after the chocolate hardens, keep at room temperature.

Index

American Cheese
  Gravy, Cheese, 130
  Grilled-Cheese Sandwich, Texas, 78
  Macaroni and, 69
  Matt's Stand-By Queso, 56
Anchovy Hollandaise Sauce, Matt's, 135
Appetizers, 1–16
  Avocado
    Caesar's Salad, 7
    and Shrimp Pico, 6
    Stuffed with Shrimp, 10
  Cactus Pod Salad, 8
  Chicken
    Gizzards, 14
    Wings, Chipotle, 4
  Chicken Livers, 15
    Starters, 9
  Green Tomatillo Gorditas, 13
  Po' Boy Crab Cakes, South Austin, 5
  Portabellos, Beefy, 2–3
  Shrimp
    Marinated, 11
    Pico, Avocado and, 6
    Skillet Scampi Texas Style, 12
    Stuffed Avocado with, 10
Arkansas Margarita, 164
Avocado
  Shrimp and
    Pico, 6
    Stuffed, 10

Bacon
  Beans, Big-Happenin', 58
  Black-Eyed Peas, New Year's Eve, 55

Gravy
  Cheese, 130
  Mesa Redondo, 133
Gumbo, Side-Dish Veggie, 52
Hominy, Fried, 51
Liver
  No. 1, 96
  Starters, 9
Oyster Miga Omelet, Midnight, 98
Po' Boy's Filet Mignon, 112
Potatoes Side Dish, Happy, 61
Red Beans and Rice No. 1, 102
Banana Eggnog with Dark Rum, What Goes
    Around Comes Around, 168–69
Barbecue Sauce
  Big Batch o', 129
  Hot Chipotle, 143
Beans
  Black Bean Chili, Beef and, 28
  Kidney
    Chili, Cajun, 23
    Red Beans and Rice No. 2, 103
  Navy, 62
  Pinto, *see* Pinto Beans
  Red
    Rice and, No. 1, 102
    Rice and, No. 2, 103
Beef
  Brisket
    Matt's Favorite Shredded, 76
    Shredded Beef (for Roasting-Range Top or
      Oven), 76
  Chili
    Black Bean and, 28
    Texas Campfire, 27

Beef (*continued*)
 Gravy, Mesa Redondo, 133
 Green Tomatillo Gorditas, 13
 Po' Boy's Filet Mignon, 112
 Portabellos, Beefy, 2–3
 Shredded
  for Crock Pots and Slow Cookers, 74
  Fajitas with, 77
  Grilled-Cheese Sandwich, Texas, 78
  for Roasting-Range-Top or Oven, 75
 Soup, Trail Blazin', 19
 Steak
  Braised Spanish, 85
  Salisbury, South Texas, 73
  Sirloin with Corn Pudding, Chili-Roasted, 92–93
 Stew with Homemade Dumplings, 29
 Tongue, 86–87
 Tripe, *see* Tripe
Beer
 Biscuits, 149
 Cornbread, 144
Best Beef Stock, The, 43
Beverages, *see* Drinks
Big Batch o' BBQ Sauce, 129
Big-Batch Potato Salad, 57
Big Dog Tartar Sauce, 128
Big-Happenin' Beans, 58
Big Mack Chicken and Rice, 114–15
Biscuits
 Beer, 149
 Matt's Favorite, 148
 Pan Loco, 150
Black Bean Chili, Beef and, 28
Black-Eyed Peas, New Year's Eve, 55
Boiled Shrimp and Shrimp Stock, 45
Bone-in, Skin-on Chicken, 82
Bourbon Coke Float, 170
Braised Spanish Steak, 85
Brandy
 Coke Float, 171
 Mediterranean Coffee, 175
 Mexican Coffee, 175

The Teeth of the Hair of the Dog That Bit You, 173
Breads, 147–58
 Biscuits
  Beer, 149
  Matt's Favorite, 148
  Pan Loco, 150
 Cornbread, 152
  Beer, 154
  Chipotle, 153
  Plain Gorditas, 157
 Gorditas
  Green Tomatillo, 13
  Plain, 157
  Spicy, 158
 Hush Puppies, 155
 Indian Fried, 156
 Pan Loco, 150
 Tortillas, Flour, 151
Broiled Soft-Shell Crabs, 72

Cactus Pod Salad, 8
Caesar's Salad, Avocado, 7
Cajun Chili, 23
Cajun Turkey Breast, 84
Caper Sauce, Dill and, 126
Cappuccino, Vanilla, 174
Catfish, Mustard, 110–11
Cheddar cheese
 Biscuits, Beer, 149
Cheese
 American, *see* American Cheese
 Cheddar
  Biscuits, Beer, 149
 Enchilada, the World's Largest, 116–18
 Monterey Jack
  Beefy Portabellos, 2–3
  Grilled-Cheese Sandwich, Hollandaise, 79
Chicken
 Breasts
  Bone-in, Skin-on, 82
  in Green Sauce with Pumpkin Seeds, 90–91

Matt's Answer to Dry, 82
  Mole, Simple, Easy, 105
Cajun, 84
Gizzards, 14
  Gumbo, Matt's Favorite, 38
  Rice, Old Time Dirty, 66
in Green Sauce with Pumpkin Seeds, 90–91
Green Tomatillo Gorditas, 13
Gumbo, Matt's Favorite, 38
Livers, *see* Chicken or Duck Livers
Pollo Guisado (Chicken and Gravy), 88–89
and Rice, Big Mack, 114–15
Stew, 32–33
Wings, Chipotle, 4
Chicken or Duck Livers, 15
  Rice, Old Time Dirty, 66
  Starters, 9
Chiles
  Ancho Sauce, Rabbit with, 100–101
  Green Chile/Jalapeño Sauce with Pork, 134
  Huevos Rancheros, Matt's Mom's, 95
  Shrimp Miga Omelet, 104
  Steak, Braised Spanish, 85
Chili, 17
  Beef
    Black Bean and, 28
    Texas Campfire, 27
  Enchilada, the World's Largest, 116–18
  Pork
    Cajun, 23
    Matt's, 25
    New Mexico, 22
  Turkey
    Cajun, 23
    Matt's Big-Time Eatin', 24
    New Mexico, 22
    South Texas, 21
    with Veggies, Matt's Big-Time Eatin',
      26
Chili-Roasted Sirloin with Corn Pudding,
  92–93
Chipotle Peppers
  Barbecue Sauce, Hot, 143

Chipotle Paste, 124
  Chicken Wings, 4
Cornbread, 153
Gorditas, Spicy, 158
Hollandaise Sauce, Matt's, 138
Jelly, 132
Sour Cream Sauce, Marco's, 141
Turkey Meatballs, Mom's, 106
Chocolate
  Atole, 172
  Sweet Dreams Tamales, 182
Chorizo
  con Huevos y Papas (Mexican Sausage with
    Eggs & Potatoes), 97
  Fideo con, 94
Cider
  Damn Hot Chocolate, 176
  Puerto Rican, 175
  Tuaca 'Bout It, 176
Coca-Cola
  Bourbon Coke Float, 170
  Rum Coke Float, 170
Coffee
  Damn Hot Chocolate, 176
  Kindred Spirit, 174
  Mediterranean, 175
  Mexican, 175
  Puerto Rican Cider, 175
  Spanish, 174
  The Teeth of the Hair of the Dog That Bit
    You, 173
  Tuaca 'Bout It, 176
  Vanilla Cappuccino, 174
Cookies, Mexican Wedding, 181
Corn
  Creamy Sweet, 67
  Gumbo
    Matt's Favorite, 38
    Side-Dish Veggie, 52
  Pudding, Chili-Roasted Sirloin with, 92–93
  Seasoned Grilled Vegetables, 68
  Soup, Cream, 20
  Summer Beans The Meal, 54

Corn *(continued)*
    Turkey Chili with Veggies, Matt's Big-Time
        Eatin', 26
Cornbread, 152
    Beer, 154
    Chipotle, 153
    Plain Gorditas, 157
Corn meal
    Catfish, Mustard, 110–11
    Cornbread, 152
      Beer, 154
      Chipotle, 153
    Hush Puppies, 155
    Oysters, Fried, 113
Crabs
    Gumbo, Seafood, 39–41
    Soft-Shell, Broiled, 72
Cream
    Quail, Wino, 108–109
    Soup, Corn, 20
Creamy Sweet Corn, 67
Custard, Sweet Potato, 177

Damn Hot Chocolate, 176
Desserts, 161, 176–82
    Cookies, Mexican Wedding, 181
    Margarita Bars, 178
    Peach Jalapeño Bars, 179
    South of the Border Granola Bars, 180
    Sweet Potato Custard, 177
    Tamales, Sweet Dreams, 182
Dill and Caper Sauce, 126
Dove & Sausage Gumbo, 37
Dressing
    French, Matt's, 140
    Thousand Island, Matt's, 139
Drinks, 161–86
    Bourbon Coke Float, 170
    Brandy Coke Float, 171
    Chocolate Atole, 172
    Coffee, *see* Coffee
    Damn Hot Chocolate, 176

Eggnog
    with Dark Rum, What Goes Around
        Comes Around Banana, 168–69
    Pumpkin, 166–67
Margarita
    Arkansas, 164
    Longhorn, 162
    Mix No. 2, 165
    Mix No. 3, 165
    Rim, Pick-Up Proof, 163
    Rum Coke Float, 170
Duck Livers, *see* Chicken or Duck Livers
Dumplings, Beef Stew with Homemade, 29

Eggnog
    with Dark Rum, What Goes Around Comes
        Around Banana, 168–69
    Pumpkin, 166–67
Eggs
    Chorizo con Huevos y Papas (Mexican
        Sausage with Eggs & Potatoes), 97
    Hollandaise Sauce
      Anchovy, Matt's, 135
      Chipotle, Matt's, 138
      Hot & Spicy, Matt's, 137
      No. 1, Matt's, 136
    Huevos Rancheros, Matt's Mom's, 95
    Margarita Bars, 178
    Miga Omelet
      Oyster, Midnight, 98
      Romantic Migas, 99
      Shrimp, 104
    Oyster Miga Omelet, Midnight, 98
    Potato Salad, Big-Batch, 57
    Tartar Sauce, Big Dog, 128
    Thousand Island Dressing, Matt's, 139
Enchilada, the World's Largest, 116–18

Fajitas with Shredded Beef, 77
Fancy Rice, 65
Fideo con Chorizo, 94

Fish, *see specific types of fish*
Flour
    for breads, *see* Breads
    Roux, Gumbo, 34–35
    Tortillas, 151
French Dressing, Matt's, 140
Fried Hominy, 51
Fried Oysters, 113
Fried Peaches No. 2, 50
Fried Spicy Okra, 59

Game Hen Gumbo, 36
Giblet Gravy for Goose or Wild Turkey,
    144–45
Goose, Giblet Gravy for, 144–45
Gorditas
    Green Tomatillo, 13
    Plain, 157
    Spicy, 158
Granola Bars, South of the Border, 180
Gravy
    Cheese, 130
    Chicken and (Pollo Guisado), 88–89
    Giblet, for Goose and Wild Turkey, 144–45
    Mesa Redondo, 133
Green Tomatillos Gorditas, 13
Gumbo, 17
    Dove & Sausage, 37
    Game Hen, 36
    Matt's Favorite, 38
    Roux, 34–35
    Seafood, 39–41
    Side-Dish Veggie, 52

Happy Potatoes Side Dish, 61
Hen Gumbo, Game, 36
Hollandaise
    Grilled-Cheese Sandwich, 79
    Sauce
      Anchovy, Matt's, 135
      Chipotle, Matt's, 138

Hot & Spicy, Matt's, 137
    No. 1, Matt's, 136
Hominy
    Chili, New Mexico, 22
    Fried, 51
    Menudo Tripe Soup (The Real Breakfast of
      Champions), 42
Hot Chipotle Barbecue Sauce, 143
Hot Dogs
    Po' Boy's Filet Mignon, 112
Hush Puppies, 155

Ice Cream, Vanilla
    Bourbon Coke Float, 170
    Brandy Coke Float, 171
    Rum Coke Float, 170
Indian Fried Bread, 156

Jalapeños
    Hush Puppies, 155
    Paste, Matt's, 122–23
    Peach Bars, 179
    Pepper Jelly, 131
    Pinto Beans, Ranch Style, 49
    Sauce with Pork, Green Chile/, 134
    Stew with Pork, New Mexican, 30
Jelly
    Chipotle Pepper, 132
    Jalapeño Pepper, 131

Kidney Beans
    Chili, Cajun, 23
    Red Beans and Rice No. 2, 103
Kindred Spirit, 174

Liver
    Calf, No. 1, 96
    Chicken or Duck, 15
      Rice, Old Time Dirty, 66

Liver (*continued*)
    Starters, 9
Longhorn Margarita, 162

Macaroni and Cheese, 69
Main courses, 71–118
Marco's Chipotle Sour Cream Sauce, 141
Margarita
    Arkansas, 164
    Bars, 178
    Longhorn, 162
    Mix No. 2, 165
    Mix No. 3, 165
    Rim, Pick-Up Proof, 163
Marinated Shrimp, 11
Masa
    Green Tomatillo Gorditas, 13
    Plain Gorditas, 157
Matt's Anchovy Hollandaise Sauce, 135
Matt's Answer to Dry Breasts, 81
Matt's Big-Time Eatin' Turkey Chili, 24
    with Veggies, 26
Matt's Chipotle Hollandaise Sauce, 138
Matt's Chipotle Paste, 124
Matt's Favorite Biscuits, 148
Matt's Favorite Gumbo, 38
Matt's Favorite Shredded Beef Brisket, 76
Matt's Jalapeño Paste, 122–23
Matt's Mom's Huevos Rancheros, 95
Matt's Pork Chili, 25
Matt's Stand-By Queso, 56
Matt's Thousand Island Dressing, 139
Matt's Turkey Balls, 107
Mayonnaise
    Tartar Sauce, Matt's Mom's, 127
    Thousand Island Dressing, Matt's, 139
Mediterranean Coffee, 175
Mesa Redondo Gravy, 133
Mexican Coffee, 175
Midnight Oyster Miga Omelet, 98
Mom's Garden Squash, 60
Mom's Turkey Meatballs, 106

Monterey Jack Cheese
    Beefy Portabellos, 2–3
    Grilled-Cheese Sandwich, Hollandaise, 79
Mushrooms
    Beefy Portabellos, 2–3
    Seasoned Grilled Vegetables, 68
Mustard Catfish, 110–11

Navy Beans, 62
New & Improved Mild Turkey Stock, 44
New Mexican Jalapeño Stew with Pork, 30
New Mexico Chili, 22
New Year's Eve Black-Eyed Peas, 55
Nopalitos
    Cactus Pod Salad, 8

Okra
    Fried Spicy, 59
    Gumbo, Side-Dish Veggie, 52
Old Time Dirty Rice, 66
Omelets, *see* Eggs
Oysters
    Fried, 113
    Gumbo, Seafood, 39–41
    Miga Omelet, Midnight, 98

Pan Loco, 150
Parsley
    Sauce, 125
    Tartar Sauce, Matt's Mom's, 127
Peaches
    Fried, No. 2, 50
    Jalapeño Bars, 179
Peanut Butter
    Chicken Mole, Simple, Easy, 105
Peas
    Black-Eyed, New Year's Eve, 55
    Sweet, 63
Pecans
    Cookies, Mexican Wedding, 181

Granola Bars, South of the Border, 180
Peach Jalapeño Bars, 179
Pickles, Dill
   Tartar Sauce
     Big Dog, 128
     Matt's Mom's, 127
Pick-Up Proof Margarita Rim, 163
Pinto Beans
   Big-Happenin', 58
   Ranch Style, 49
   Summer Beans The Meal, 54
   Taste-the-Goodness, 53
   Whole, 48
Plain Gorditas, 157
Plain Rice, 64
Po' Boy Crab Cakes, South Austin, 5
Po' Boy's Filet Mignon, 112
Pollo Guisado (Chicken and Gravy), 88–89
Pork
   Chili, *see* Chili, Pork
   Chops, Red Pork No. 1, 80
   Green Chile/Jalapeño Sauce with, 134
   Green Tomatillo Gorditas, 13
   Rinds
     Arkansas Margarita, 164
     Pinto Beans, Ranch Style, 49
   Salt Pork, *see* Salt Pork
   Sausage, *see* Sausage
   Stew with, New Mexican Jalapeño, 30
Portabellos, Beefy, 2–3
Potato(es)
   Salad, Big-Batch, 57
   Sausage with Eggs and, Mexican, 97
   Side Dish, Happy, 61
Poultry, *see specific types of poultry, e.g.* Chicken;
   Game Hen
Pudding, Chili-Roasted Sirloin with Corn,
   92–93
Puerto Rican Cider, 175
Pumpkin
   Eggnog, 166–67
   Seeds, Chicken in Green Sauce with, 90–91

Quail, Wino, 108–109

Rabbit
   with Chile Ancho Sauce, 100–101
   Stew, 32–33
Real Breakfast of Champions (Menudo Tripe
   Soup), 42
Red Beans and Rice No. 1, 102
Red Pork No. 1, 80
Rice
   Chicken and, Big Mack, 114–15
   Dirty, Old Time, 66
   Fancy, 65
   Plain, 64
   Red Beans and
     No. 1, 102
     No. 2, 103
Romantic Migas, 99
Roux, Gumbo, 34–35
Rum
   Coke Float, 170
   Puerto Rican Cider, 175
   What Goes Around, Comes Around Banana
     Eggnog with Dark, 168–69

Salad
   Cactus Pod, 8
   Caesar's, Avocado, 7
   Potato, Big-Batch, 57
Salmon
   Po' Boy Crab Cakes, South Austin, 5
Salt Pork
   Beans, Taste-the-Goodness, 53
   Navy Beans, 62
   Pinto Beans, Whole, 48
   Red Beans and Rice
     No. 1, 102
     No. 2, 103
   Summer Beans The Meal, 54
Sandwiches, Grilled-Cheese
   Hollandaise, 79

Sandwiches, Grilled-Cheese (continued)
    Texas, 78
Sauces, see Toppings and Sauces
Sausage
    Chorizo
        con Huevos y Papas (Mexican Sausage
            with Eggs & Potatoes), 97
        Fideo con, 94
        Gravy, Mesa Redondo, 133
        Gumbo, Dove &, 37
    Seafood
        Gumbo, 39–41
        see also specific types of seafood
Seasoned Grilled Vegetables, 68
Shredded Beef, see Beef, Shredded
Shrimp
    Avocado with
        Pico, 6
        Stuffed, 10
    Gumbo, Seafood, 39–41
    Marinated, 11
    Miga Omelet, 104
    Skillet Scampi Texas Style, 12
    Stew, 31
    Stock, Boiled Shrimp and, 45
Side dishes, 47–69
Side-Dish Veggie Gumbo, 52
Simple, Easy Chicken Mole, 105
Slow-Cooked Turkey Breast, 83
Sopa de Fideo (Vermicelli), 18
Soups, 17
    Beef, Trail Blazin', 19
    Corn, Cream, 20
    Menudo Tripe (The Real Breakfast of Cham-
        pions), 42
    Sopa de Fideo (Vermicelli), 18
    Stock, see Stock
Sour Cream Sauce
    Marco's Chipotle, 141
    Marco's No. 1, 142
South Austin Po' Boy Crab Cakes, 5
South of the Border Granola Bars, 180
South Texas Chili, 21

South Texas Salisbury Steak, 73
Spanish Coffee, 174
Spicy Gorditas, 13
Squash
    Yellow
        Seasoned Grilled Vegetables, 68
    Zucchini, see Zucchini
Steak, see Beef, Steak
Stew, 17
    Beef, with Homemade Dumplings, 29
    Pork, New Mexican Jalapeño Stew with, 30
    Rabbit, 32–33
    Shrimp, 31
Stock, 17
    Beef, The Best, 43
    Shrimp, Boiled Shrimp and, 45
    Turkey, New & Improved Mild, 44
Stuffed Avocado with Shrimp, 10
Summer Beans The Meal, 54
Sweet Peas, 63
Sweet Potato Custard, 177

Tamales, Sweet Dreams, 182
Tartar Sauce
    Big Dog, 128
    Matt's Mom's, 127
Taste-of-Goodness Beans, 53
Teeth of the Hair of the Dog That Bit You, The,
    173
Tequila
    Margarita Mix No. 2, 165
    Margarita Mix No. 3, 165
Texas Campfire Chili, 27
Texas Grilled-Cheese Sandwich, 78
Thousand Island Dressing, Matt's, 139
Tomatillos
    Chicken in Green Sauce with Pumpkin
        Seeds, 90–91
    Green, Gorditas, 13
Tongue, Beef, 86–87
Toppings and Sauces, 121–45
    Anchovy Hollandaise, Matt's, 135

Barbecue Sauce
   Big Batch o', 129
   Hot Chipotle, 143
Chipotle
   Barbecue Sauce, Hot, 143
   Paste, 124
   Sour Cream Sauce, Marco's, 141
Dill and Caper, 126
French Dressing, Matt's, 140
Gravy, *see* Gravy
Green Chile/Jalapeño, with Pork, 134
Hollandaise
   Chipotle, Matt's, 138
   Hot & Spicy, Matt's, 137
   Matt's Anchovy, 135
   No. 1, Matt's, 136
Jalapeño Paste, Matt's, 122–23
Jelly
   Chipotle Pepper, 132
   Jalapeño Pepper, 131
Parsley, 125
Sour Cream
   Chipotle, Marco's, 141
   Marco's No. 1, 142
Tartar
   Big Dog, 128
   Matt's Mom's, 127
Thousand Island Dressing, Matt's, 139
Tortillas
   Enchilada, the World's Largest, 116–18
   Flour, 151
   Migas, Romantic, 99
   Oyster Miga Omelet, Midnight, 98
   Shrimp Miga Omelet, 104
Tripe Soup, Menudo (The Real Breakfast of
   Champions), 42
Tuaca 'Bout It, 176
Turkey
   Balls, Matt's, 107

Breast
   Cajun, 84
   Slow-Cooked, 83
Chili, *see* Chili, Turkey
Meatballs, Mom's, 106
Stock, New & Improved Mild, 44
Wild, Giblet Gravy for, 144–45

Vanilla Cappuccino, 174
Vanilla Ice Cream
   Bourbon Coke Float, 170
   Brandy Coke Float, 171
   Rum Coke Float, 170
Vegetables
   Gumbo, Side-Dish Veggie, 52
   Rice, Fancy, 65
   Seasoned Grilled, 68
   Turkey Chili with, Matt's Big-Time Eatin', 26
   see also specific vegetabls
Venison
   Gravy, Mesa Redondo, 133
Vermicelli
   Fideo con Chorizo, 94
   Sopa de Fideo, 94

Whole Pinto Beans, 48
Wino Quail, 108–109

Zucchini
   Gumbo, Matt's Favorite, 38
   Mom's Garden Squash, 60
   Seasoned Grilled Vegetables, 68
   Summer Beans The Meal, 54
   Turkey Chili with Veggies, Matt's Big-Time
    Eatin', 26